Praise for *Resume Secrets for Recent Grads*

"Chris shines a light on areas I was unaware were holding me back. As soon as I incorporated his advice I was able to land my dream job. His advice is timeless and will continue to open doors for me in the future."

- Omar Rodriguez, Research Analyst

"Chris polished some of the blemishes within my professional image and rebuilt my resume from simply describing what I do into where I make an impact. He helped me change my lexicon in more of an applied manner so it resonates."

- Joseph Sahili, Human Capital Consultant

As you rework your resume, do me a favor and email me
your ideas, comments, and suggestions.
I want to know what you think.

ResumeSecretsBook@gmail.com

Access additional content at:
www.ResumeSecretsBook.com

Dedicated to the greatest woman alive:

My mother.

Love you mom.

Resume Secrets for Recent Grads

Proven strategies to land interviews

Chris Munshaw

Table of Contents

Part One

Part Two

Part One

Foreword

I hate to be the one to burst your bubble, but if you are searching for a job, here are two hard truths you must face: First, HR managers aren't combing through every résumé to find the best candidate and second, you are not that special. In this era of corporate consolidation and automation, most human resources departments are understaffed and overworked. The result is 98.2% of Fortune 500 companies are using Application Tracking Systems to quickly scan resumes and fill openings. Recruiters aren't bonused for hiring the best; they are rewarded for filling vacancies quickly.

As a former NASDAQ company CEO and a senior executive with multinational corporations that hire hundreds of thousands of employees, I can share with you what the hiring experience looks like from the employer's point-of-view. By the time a new job is budgeted for, the company needed that employee to start months ago. Smart managers know to fill their headcount quickly before the next hiring freeze or downsizing eliminates the position and increases their workload. The average job that is posted online attracts around 250 résumés of which less than six will be called in for an interview. More than half of the résumés submitted are passed over by ATS software and never read by a human. Your resume is just raw data being scored by an algorithm.

Even more daunting is the fact that nearly 80% of all jobs are never even listed online. Jobs are filled through networking as quickly as possible. When I started working with Reid Hoffman on LinkedIn in 2006, we recognized the importance of networking through carefully-crafted public profiles and what a powerful tool it could become for jobseekers. To employers, how you present yourself online can be as important as what you write on your résumé.

Secondly, as a recent college graduate, you aren't that special. Your value to employers will grow with your experience and accomplishments, but for now you are one of 1.8 million students who graduated from an American university this year. Looking for a job with a large multinational? The odds are even worse as you will also be competing against the 8 million Chinese students and 9 million Indian students who also graduated this year (not to mention students from countless other universities around the globe). The good news is that you have a strategic advantage over the vast majority of these recent graduates (and you are holding it in your hands right now).

Chris Munshaw has meticulously broken down and demystified the job hiring process to arm you with the best tools for increasing your odds of not only getting hired, but getting hired for the job you really want. In my book *Disrupt You!*, I wrote: "The most important tool you have on a résumé is language." *Resume Secrets for Recent Grads* will show you the words to use to get noticed and hired. To truly stand out, candidates need to focus on personal branding and become a brand of one. Munshaw's book goes beyond mere language and highlights the psychology behind formatting your résumé and making it visually pop (in a professional way).

As Artificial Intelligence tools become cheaper, more small companies will be using software to select candidates. Even knowing this fact, most people still put more effort into selecting a restaurant from Yelp than they do into polishing their personal brand and accelerating their career. Put in the effort now and reap the rewards over your lifetime.

Getting hired isn't a one-time task. You will come back to use the tools in this book again and again throughout your career. Whether by choice or circumstance, every career gets disrupted. The average tenure for new employees at Google, Apple, and Facebook is less than two years! You can passively let your career happen or take charge of your life and plan for success.

Your career choices come down to one existential question: Would you rather work forty hours a week at a job you hate or eighty hours a week doing work you love? The real challenge for each of us is to determine where we feel we can make the most impact. I firmly believe that the purpose of life is to live a life of purpose. Go after a job that fulfills your purpose. Nothing is more rewarding than the satisfaction of making a positive difference with your life. But you won't be able to change the world or have a global impact without getting onto the first rung of the ladder. Use *Resume Secrets for Recent Grads* as your step stool to get started.

Jay Samit

Introduction

"Life is in the transitions..." - William James

There is a glaring problem that colleges and universities fail to take seriously. Whether it's community college or graduate school, recent graduates are struggling.

Here's the reality: you just spent a considerable amount of time and money on your education, and you've graduated into a job market that averages seven months before landing a job[1]... and that's just the average. About 83% of graduates leave school without first lining up a job.[2] As of the writing of this book, the current alternative unemployment rate in the U.S. is nearly 21%.[3]

Based on a salary of $4,000 a month, the average graduate loses $29,600 during the job search compared to the graduate who steps into a job immediately after receiving a degree.[4] That's enough for the Class of 2019 to pay back three-fourths of its student loans.

Good times, right?

Does the following sound familiar: you open an email in the hopes of getting an interview but it turns out to be a standard

---

[1] https://www.naceweb.org/

[2] https://www.washington.edu/doit/what-can-students-do-improve-their-chances-finding-employment-after-college

[3] http://www.shadowstats.com/alternate_data/unemployment-charts
While the alternative unemployment rate is debatable, the Bureau of Labor and Statistics (BLS) list national unemployment at 3.7%. I specifically state the alternative figure as the BLS figure fails to account for discouraged workers and is misleading.

[4] https://www.washington.edu/doit/what-can-students-do-improve-their-chances-finding-employment-after-college

rejection email saying something along the lines of, *"Thank you for applying, but we went with another candidate. We'll keep your resume on file should a better fit open up."*

Here is another bit of reality to consider: many companies' hiring processes are run by hiring managers with little HR training. [5] I have my opinions about this, but that's beyond the scope of this book.

The way that employers seek employees is constantly evolving. In fact, let me make a little prediction: 10 years from now, resumes will be as irrelevant or useful as CD players are today. By then your work history, experience, skills, and education will all be validated upon digital credentialing through blockchain technology.[6] Until then, though, society will be stuck with resumes.

That is the reason for this book. It is for you. Why not make your resume stand out? I designed it to be the ultimate DIY resume builder for recent grads. It's the book I wish I'd had.

If you are reading this, I suspect you were once like me, banging your head against the wall when applying for jobs, wondering why no one would call you back, and blaming yourself for this situation.

Out of nothing but a senseless feeling of self-shame I'd blame myself for lacking in some skill and that was the reason why no one wanted to hire me. I'd make up the most outlandish theories for why hiring managers weren't calling me. Despite

---

[5] https://www.theatlantic.com/health/archive/2019/06/looking-for-a-job-americas-listings-are-inscrutable/591616/

[6] https://www.learningmachine.com/credential-n/
"Blockcerts.org — the open standard for securing digital records by using a blockchain as a global notary system to verify authenticity. The goal of this resource is to provide people with the ability to store their own records and use them directly in the world when they see fit. Further, relying parties can use the open-source verifier to instantly check these credentials, a process that generates a hash of the local document and compares it to a hash on the blockchain. When everything matches, and it has not expired or been revoked, the credential is verified."

feeling that I was somehow inadequate, I'd tell myself things like

"Hey Chris, you're willing to learn and you're a hard worker... so what could really be wrong with you? Any employer would be lucky to have you on their staff!"

Still, giving myself pep talks wasn't enough. It wasn't until years later, after spending thousands of dollars and years studying marketing and resumes from the best around, that I started to figure out what was really going on. I realized that not only was my approach to resumes, interviews, and employment completely wrong, the way I was thinking about resumes, the job search, and how to market myself was wrong, too.

What gives me the authority to write such a book like this?

The secrets in this book work because grads have reported back to me that they've secured interviews and landed jobs. Some admittedly take a little bit longer than others, but these secret strategies get them to the promise land.

After landing several positions that I truly wanted in my career I discovered the subtle edits and structural changes that had to be made not just to my resume and approach, but to my mindset, too.

I hired resume writers from well-known job boards, thinking they would be the answer to my prayers. Oh man, was I wrong. Popular resume sites (resume mills) regurgitated my words but in a prettier font. I put those resumes out to an A/B split test and the results were negligible.

Two experts who taught me a ton and deserve attribution are Ross MacPherson of Your Career Quest and John Suarez of the Professional Association of Resume Writers & Career Coaches.

Despite their wise instruction I continued studying dozens of books on branding, advice from resume writers, books on marketing, advertising, copywriting, interviewed hiring managers from Fortune 500 companies, and talked to human resource reps about their views of the best practices for resumes. I'll be sharing many of these secrets with you here.

Funny enough, early in my career I landed a job that had me reviewing other people's resumes, too. So I was an expert on resume style, right? Negative. Unfortunately there was no corporate resume review class.

Well, I was definitely getting closer to having a better understanding of resumes and self-branding and why some candidates advanced and others didn't, but I still needed to learn quite a bit more even though I was a hiring manager. I had been on the job only a few months and had moved from a state of complete mental desperation to find a job to suddenly having the responsibility of reviewing dozens of resumes, many of which I couldn't bear to read (it's amazing how many applicants say they are *proficient* at MS Word!) even though I was very empathetic towards the situations of those job applicants. I wish I could have given everyone a shot, but of course I couldn't. I'm thankful for this experience because it gave me a much better understanding of the hiring process from both sides.

I saw firsthand how Applicant Tracking System (ATS) software organized and filtered candidates. I saw how rejections could happen as fast as a mouse click—and how easy it was to move a candidate forward to schedule an interview. This discovery of how disposable job candidates are infuriated me but also helped me understand that it was silly for me to have taken the process so personally before. I was one of those candidates, yet I was blind to the mistakes I was making. It was the equivalent of feeling insulted when a traffic light changes. I was getting upset because I wasn't receiving the results I wanted, yet I assumed I understood the process when in reality I had no idea.

In *Resume Secrets for Recent Grads* I will share some very practical lessons from my experience as a candidate, a hiring manager, and helping grads that can be applied today. I have also removed much of the marketing theory and strategy background of modern resumes so that you can simply focus on these tips and approaches and make changes as you see fit. If I tried to pack in all of the marketing theory, this would end up being a full-on textbook. I'm not interested in a snooze fest.

Even without that additional material, these strategies should not be rushed. Read this book slowly and carefully. Some readers won't want to do that. When they have a rough idea of how to write their resumes, they rush through the process just to get it out, and that often results in a clumsy cut-and-paste job. It's no wonder people don't like putting together their resumes. It's the equivalent of eating an egg before it's cooked … no thank you! So, regardless of how quickly you want to rush through this book and skip ahead, I urge you to please study all of the material carefully. Your time to employment and earning potential depends upon it.

You'll also notice that <u>I choose not to spell resume with the French spelling of résumé.</u> I suppose that's my rebellious streak of wanting to do things my own way. My book, my rules. I appreciate the cultural essence and etymology of the word, but at this point the context will inform you, the reader, about the way the word is being used of which is already implied. For example: *I like a caramelized date. I went out on a date. My date of birth...* you get the idea. What about the accents? Outside of French-speaking regions I find it rare to see accents on other common French words that we've adopted into English: cafe, fiance, cliche, risque, or touche. So I'm taking a stand that we can do the same with RESUME. What do you think? Fantastic! I'm glad you're on board with me.

I've divided this glorious adventure into two parts. Part one is practical by design and aims to have you think differently about your resume in order to take action and see results. Part two is filled with bonus strategies to help keep you competitive... or put you to sleep. I'll let you decide.

Recent graduates can sometimes be perceived in the job market as career changers after spending a bit of time completing coursework, and that's why it's important to study the strategies in the following pages. Modern resumes and LinkedIn profiles are nothing more than personalized marketing campaigns. Some read by robots and others are not. More about that later. And some will argue that a resume is a waste of time and to center your attention only on your LinkedIn profile. Granted, since we are in a digital age, Google will still ask you for your resume when applying to anyone of their roles. When comparing candidates I've bypassed resumes without a LinkedIn profile or complementary portfolio of work. **A resume is necessary but no longer sufficient by itself.** Go back and reread that sentence again.

A final word about mindset before we begin: Without the right thought process to get through this, none of what follows will work effectively for you even if you have an amazing resume. HR reps and hiring managers hire candidates they know, like, and trust. That's so important that it's worth saying again: **Hiring managers hire candidates they know, like, and trust.** The greatest risk to your resume is your mindset and how you approach it, write it, the examples you choose, and the phrases that you copy and borrow. Private victories will precede public ones. Staying optimistic will give you the mental power to consistently perform the task, keep focused, and have the bandwidth to get through those moments when you feel that you are being ignored or rejected.

The most important thing I can tell you about mindset is this: You are not alone. You need to know that people like me are here to help support you in your efforts and goals. Knowing— and believing—that this is true will give you the confidence to reach out for help and accept it. When you are optimistic about your resume and the job hunt, you realize that failure isn't a constant: it's nothing but a data point, a piece of feedback, and nothing else. No single failure scenario defines you; rather, it creates more awareness about new areas of opportunity and how to improve yourself. Embrace the belief that, despite roadblocks, the labor market, or the company, you will always find a way!

Prior to winning three Academy Awards, Steven Spielberg was rejected by the University of Southern California several times.[7] Before Jay Leno got his start was he arrested for vagrancy twice, which was ironically near where his Hollywood star is today.[8] They found a way and so can you.

---

[7] https://www.cbsnews.com/pictures/celebs-who-went-from-failures-to-success-stories/9/

[8] https://www.yahoo.com/entertainment/blogs/tv-news/jay-leno-television-academy-hall-of-fame-induction-190110392.html

Just the way an art student sees three lines, I'm going to change the way you look at resumes from now on.

(Hint: the negative space in between the lines is also a line)

So, let's get to it!

Chapter 1 Laying the Foundation

The hiring process is broken. It has been broken for a long time, and it will probably stay that way... unless you're "in the know" of making it work for you... unless you choose to learn the secrets in this book.

Modern hiring no longer comes down to a single person but rather a full committee. Just because you might be the first of 15 applications on LinkedIn or you happen to know the hiring manager and think you've secured an interview so there's no need to make an effort with your resume — negative. Don't let that type of thinking cloud your thought process; it's quite the contrary. You have more people to impress in a shorter period of time ... but that doesn't mean it can't be done!

I have some good news to share with you: Most resumes and LinkedIn profiles are GARBAGE. They are incredibly boring. Why is that good news? It means that yours doesn't have to be. In general, there are two basic resume styles: 1) for creatives that contain graphics and designs and 2) for corporate and business situations. I will be focusing on the latter. If you have a creative resume, though, the strategies I will share still apply.

Stop reading right now if you don't believe that you can follow these <u>three mandatory rules</u> when it comes to your resume(s):

Fix all spelling errors and grammatical mistakes.

Don't lie or even stretch the truth.

Try not to rush through the process.

> *"People do more research when buying a flat-screen TV or a washing machine than when they're looking for a job."*
> - Gary Burnison, CEO of Korn/Ferry International

When you lied on your resume about previously having sheepdog experience

Hiring Manager: It says on your resume that you went to Harvard University

Me: Yeah, I was visiting a friend

Your resume...

Submitting your resume everywhere

These memes are a bit cheeky, but there is some truth to them in suggesting the lengths to which job seekers will go when they are under the financial pressures of paying rent and student loans.

That desperation is understandable, but if you are unable to adhere to those three mandatory rules just given above, stop right here. I mean it! There is no reason to continue reading if you don't.

If you do, well then, please continue.

When was the last time that you read a LinkedIn profile or resume that was so compelling you thought, *"WOW! I'd hire that person any day!"* I'm willing to bet you never have.

Why not?

Your LinkedIn profile and resume, at BEST, get looked at for between five and 10 seconds. That's it. But even then they're being scanned and not thoroughly studied. That means that those first few seconds are critical. If you don't powerfully— and quickly—demonstrate your value, you'll lose them. It's that simple. We MUST be laser-focused on who we are and what we're after. Your resume and LinkedIn profile both demonstrate to HR recruiters and hiring managers that you possess an ability to present your skills, write effectively, and clearly organize your thoughts and structure them collectively.

The best way to demonstrate this ability is by not wasting time. State your intention with your job title and headline at the top, front and center. With all the alerts, messages, and advertisements jockeying for our attention each day it's vital to capture hiring managers attention as well as make it past the ATS. The top-third (your headline) is the marketing for your LinkedIn profile and your resume. I'll expand more on this in Chapter 8, but just know that it's the advertisement for the advertisement we use to capture their attention. Most of us, by nature, are skimmers, and it's no wonder with all the information that's attacking us on a daily basis. We have to filter through it all. That's just what hiring managers and HR reps do, too. You only have a few seconds at most to capture their attention, so you need to communicate a powerful result IMMEDIATELY. Every word is money when writing your LinkedIn profile and resume. And here's something that some people don't realize: The content cannot be the same for both.

Your LinkedIn profile is there to complement your resume and vice versa.

Your resume is ONLY designed to get you in the door — that's it. Once you're on HR's select list of filtered candidates, the resume has done its job. From there, the rest is up to you and how you market yourself 1) by phone or email (usually both) 2) in person.

In my experience on both sides of the table as a hiring manager and a job candidate I would estimate that your resume and LinkedIn profile make up a fair portion of the journey from applying to receiving an offer. Once you have your foot in the door, though, your success largely comes down to how you're able to market yourself over the phone and in person.

*Not inclusive of every step in the process

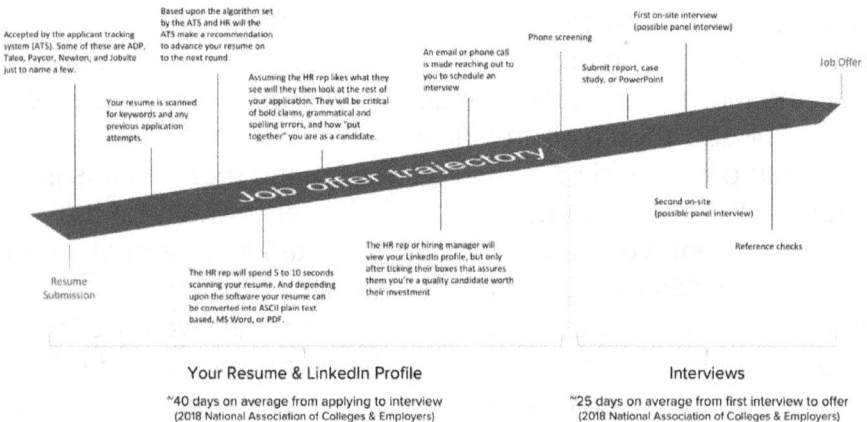

Job offer trajectory

Accepted by the applicant tracking system (ATS). Some of these are ADP, Taleo, Paycor, Newton, and Jobvite just to name a few.

Based upon the algorithm set by the ATS and HR will the ATS make a recommendation to advance your resume on to the next round.

Your resume is scanned for keywords and any previous application attempts.

Assuming the HR rep likes what they see will they then look at the rest of your application. They will be critical of bold claims, grammatical and spelling errors, and how "put together" you are as a candidate.

An email or phone call is made reaching out to you to schedule an interview

Phone screening

First on-site interview (possible panel interview)

Submit report, case study, or PowerPoint

Job Offer

Second on-site (possible panel interview)

Reference checks

Resume Submission

The HR rep will spend 5 to 10 seconds scanning your resume. And depending upon the software your resume can be converted into ASCII plain text based, MS Word, or PDF.

The HR rep or hiring manager will view your LinkedIn profile, but only after ticking their boxes that assures them you're a quality candidate worth their investment

Your Resume & LinkedIn Profile
~40 days on average from applying to interview
(2018 National Association of Colleges & Employers)

Interviews
~25 days on average from first interview to offer
(2018 National Association of Colleges & Employers)

On average it takes 65 days from applying to receiving an offer.[9] Did you know this? Did you realize how crucial your

[9] https://www.naceweb.org/talent-acquisition/candidate-selection/employers-prefer-candidates-with-work-experience/

resume and LinkedIn profile are in the job hunt? That is why it is really hard to stand out if you, your resume, and your LinkedIn profile look like everyone else's. Not only do you have to look better, you have to demonstrate credibility, too. We are NOT interested in rudimentary resumes or cut-and-paste strategies from Google or your friend's brother's resume. Instead, we are interested in making sure that your profile leaps out of the pack. This is as much about separating yourself from the rest as it is about branding yourself. Keep the following point in mind:

A resume for everyone rarely reaches anyone.

Imagine for a second that you have a headache (hopefully you don't), and you go down to your local store to pick up something for your headache. Very likely you'll go for something specific like Tylenol, Advil, or Aleve—known brand names for headache medication. While shopping, however, you notice a box labeled "medicine." Would you pick it up instead? Likely not. Why? Because you want something that is going to specifically solve the pain of your headache, not something generically labeled as medicine. Who knows what the box of medicine solves, and who cares! You want results: so you grab the Tylenol and move on about your day. The same is true for you and your resume.

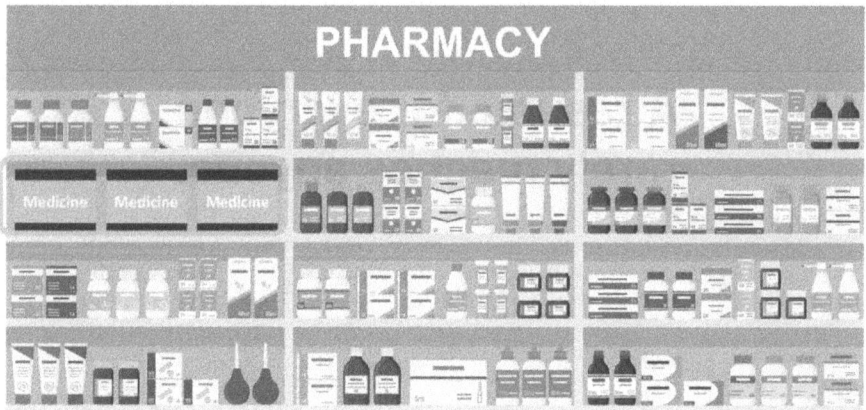

There is no such thing as an effective generic resume. Firms rarely hire generic people. The companies that interest you want specialists: They want experts who are good at what they do. Companies are willing to accept hundreds (if not thousands) of applicants because they know how to filter through them to find their specialist. Often it's a numbers game.

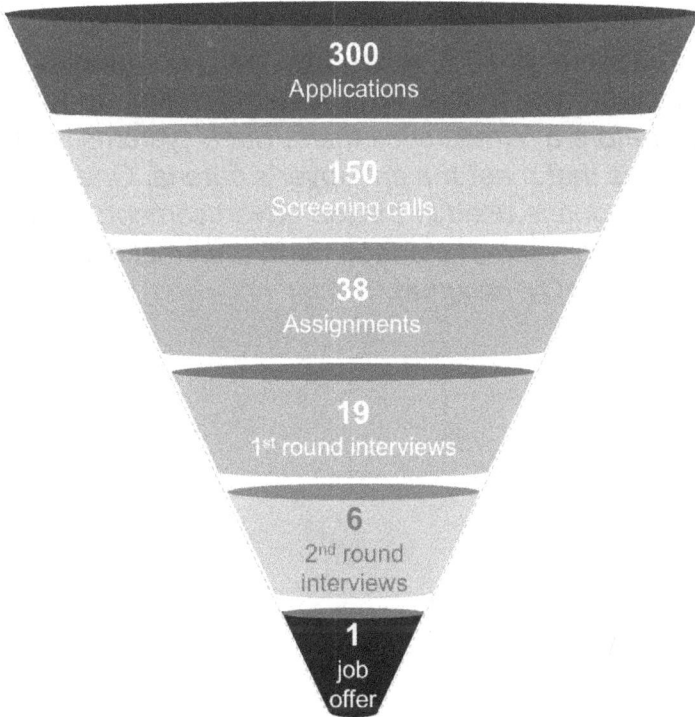

An example of the competitive landscape for one job.

300 Applications
150 Screening calls
38 Assignments
19 1st round interviews
6 2nd round interviews
1 job offer

Given this funnel, it's no surprise that more than 43 percent of graduates are underemployed.[10] That means that graduates are not earning their full potential or have not found roles that utilize their skills.

In the introduction, I mentioned that Applicant Tracking System software, or ATS, is used by many companies to filter countless resumes. In fact, ATS systems *"reject up to 75% of resumes before a human sees them. Such systems are hunting for keywords that meet the employer's criteria. One tip is to study the language used in the job advertisement; if the initials PM are used for project management, then make sure PM appears in your CV [resume]."*[11]

[10] https://www.burning-glass.com/wp- content/uploads/permanent_detour_underemployment_report.pdf
[11] "How An Algorithm May Decide Your Career," *Economist,* June, 21, 2018.
https://www.economist.com/business/2018/06/21/how-an-algorithm-may-decide-your-career

Chapter 2 What Your Resume is Not

I want to share a secret with you about your resume:

Your resume is not for you.

Surprised? Although it certainly is ABOUT you, your resume is for the recruiter and your future hiring manager — not you.

Here is another important secret:

Your resume isn't set in stone.

It is imperative that you tailor your resume for every job. Isn't that a lot of work? Yes, it can be at first, which is why people often wonder why they never hear back from the companies that they've approached. It actually isn't that much work to adjust your resume's content once you get used to doing it. Often, when the topic of resumes comes up, students have complained to me that they sent their resumes to dozens, if not hundreds, of job openings without a single response. Not surprising. Out of school I took a similar approach and I can remember my mom telling me over the phone, *"You better hurry up and apply to lots of jobs!"* Then the following conversation would start off, *"How many applications did you get in?"* Advice that meant well unfortunately didn't translate into results.

Why not? Because I, like many others followed the same approach with a single, standard version of our professional backgrounds rather than carefully crafting it for each role and for similar roles. It's not a high numbers game to shout from the mountain top and pray that someone will hear you. Rather, it's a low numbers approach to narrow the field and customize your resume for each position. The simple fact that you're taking the time to tweak and revise your content (even just a little bit) gives you an advantage because, guess what everyone else is doing? Sending out the same dull resumes to everyone and anyone with an email address. I get it. You want the satisfaction of putting numbers on the board to say you've applied to X number of jobs and feel like you're being productive. No doubt. Yet, scrambling for any job is only satisfying your short-term emotions while sacrificing your long-term career goals.

If you find yourself in a tight spot and need a temp job to hold you over – I get that. Just be critical of yourself to not stay there too long. Your future self needs you to get on your path so you can learn before you earn.

Hiring Manager Psychology

As a hiring manager I'm looking for a combination of the following: Are you easy to work with? How well do you work with others? Are you coachable? Does your specialized skill set help me solve a problem? What evidence do you have (blog, conference paper, speaking engagement, etc.) that can demonstrate you have an opinion about the industry and can speak to your excitement about wanting to learn more? Do you live close by? Are you planning on staying in the role for a while? Selfish? Yes. But that's the reality of many hiring managers is they want to know what you can do for them. This is a big contrast when most resumes just regurgitate their old job descriptions and hope that will suffice.

Also, what are you doing to feed your mind? Do you voluntarily go to conferences about the topic you're interested in? Have you read the top five, or, for the ambitious types, the top 20 books on Amazon in your field? Do you seek out mentors in your industry? If you have, I'd certainly want to know about it.

Warren Buffett has said that reading changed his life.[12] Interestingly enough, when he was 19 he read *The Intelligent Investor* and that cemented his decision to dedicate his life to investing. One book, read at the right time, literally returned billions of dollars in his lifetime.[13]

Even listing the books you've read demonstrates your interests and that you're not faking it. Mega CEO Elon Musk says several books have shaped his life the most, and that has been one of the factors in allowing him to be so versatile and to do what he does.[14] Beyond flexing your reading prowess, don't be

---

[12] https://www.cnbc.com/2017/02/02/billionaire-warren-buffett-discusses-the-book-that-changed-his-life.html
[13] https://dailystoic.com/Read
[14] https://www.businessinsider.com/books-elon-musk-thinks-everyone-should-read-2018-4

surprised to find that the HR rep or hiring manager has also read at least one of the books you've listed. You're now more relatable and building rapport to set yourself apart from the other candidates.

If you're short on time to get the gist of a book, I suggest a visit to Blinkist.com and listen at 2x the listening speed.

The image on the right is illustrative of what happens to a hiring manager's mind when a resume isn't tailored for the role. They are left to fill in the gaps for themselves.

Some people see a head and shoulders, others see a baby. What do you see? Hopefully you see a person on a horse.

So just like your resume, if your skills are not fully communicated do you risk leaving the hiring manager to fill in the blanks for themselves, which can sometimes be unusual assumptions, and more often than not is discarded all together.

(Image source: Roy Street, Gestalt Completion Test, Teachers College, Columbia University)

If you apply for several jobs outside your area of expertise at the same company, you run the risk of being snubbed.

You might not think it's a big deal to send the same resume to everyone. How will they know? Trust me: They will! Seasoned HR reps and hiring managers not only see the difference between a tailored resume and a resume that was sent out blindly, they also can tell from your resume if you're serious

---

[15] https://www.researchgate.net/publication/44569219_Construal-Level_Theory_of_Psychological_Distance#pf6

about landing the job or not. The difference is a list of facts and responsibilities on a resume (boring!) vs. your narrative on a resume that aligns well with the job description.

When you apply to more than two roles at the same company, this instantly puts your hiring manager in a tough position. Why? Because it is likely that one hiring manager will reject you for a role because you're unqualified, and even though you are more qualified for another role the hiring manager for that position will have to deal with internal politics caused by your applying and being rejected for the other position. For whatever reason a hiring manager rejected you for role A but you're better-suited for role B and that will put the two hiring managers at odds. Unless there is a clear overlap between two roles, applying for both should be made with caution.

Even if you find that you're lacking a certain skill set for the role you're interested in, don't discount yourself. Get as close to it as you can by reading up on the topic, watching YouTube videos, and blogging about it. Take a Coursera or Udacity class. Skill-based certificates are the quickest path to employment and promotion.[16] If the position requires three years' experience and you only have two, that is fine. Demonstrate that anyways. Don't write yourself off. I can look past three years' experience if you have ambition, help me solve a problem, and are easy to work with. This is why you need to go deep in studying the role and studying the hiring manager.

Don't make the tired and overworked hiring manager hunt, research, or guess how wonderful you are: Tell them in your resume.

---

[16] https://medium.com/@Chrismunshaw/the-largest-educational-system-in-the-us-is-profiting-off-of-students-fragilities-rather-than-7b19514cbe8

Here is a great perspective from Ryan Holiday in his book *The Obstacle is the Way*:

> *George Clooney spent his first years in Hollywood getting rejected at auditions. He wanted the producers and directors to like him, but they didn't and it hurt and he blamed the system for not seeing how good he was. Yet, everything changed for George when he tried a new perspective. He realized that casting is an obstacle for producers, too — they need to find somebody, and they're all hoping that the next person to walk in the room is the right somebody. Auditions were a chance to solve their problem, not his.*
>
> *From George's new perspective, he became the solution. He wasn't someone groveling for a shot. He was someone with something special to offer. He was the answer to their prayers, not the other way around. That was what he began projecting in his auditions — not exclusively his acting skills but that he was the man for the job. That he understood what the casting director and producers were looking for in a specific role and that he would deliver it in each and every situation, in preproduction, on camera, and during promotion.*[17]

Just as Clooney shifted his perspective to solve his audience's problem, you should do the same thing as you prepare your resume.

---

[17] The Obstacle Is the Way: The Timeless Art of Turning Trials into Triumph, by Ryan Holiday

> *"If there is any one secret of success, it lies in the ability to get the other person's point of view and see things from that person's angle as well as from your own."*
> - Dale Carnegie

But What About Your Experience?

Maybe you feel you don't have enough experience. How you position yourself can often make up for experience. Wait, what? What is this magic I speak of? Let me explain.

Empathy is a persuasive thing. In short, if you can describe the hiring manager's problem better than he or she can — then you've got them. That's it. You've got them. Try to think back to the last time you fully felt understood. I'm willing to bet it's only been a handful of times in your life. I mean truly feeling understood is quite rare, so when it happens does it create an emotional bond that's powerful enough to override logic. This is where empathy in understanding what's keeping the hiring manager up at night can reign supreme. So, how do you describe the hiring manager's problem *better* than he or she can?

You do this by studying up on the hiring manager. Study their background, where they went to school, their hobbies, and what they blog about. Take him or her out to coffee. Connect with other team members in the same department and also invite them out to coffee. Build rapport with the hiring manager and the team members and ask what some of their biggest challenges are. Don't expect to get state secrets or anything, yet by leveraging their responses - use the same words used to describe their pain - on your resume will that set you apart. You will need to go deep here in capturing the frustration not just from the hiring manager, team members, and company, but also the industry.

Interesting side note - the deeper you understand their problem, know what the hiring manager values, and how to solve the pain of the problem - the more leverage you will have in negotiations.

When you describe your hiring manager's problem better than he or she can, and show examples of how you already solved their problem, **your perceived lack of experience is no longer an issue.** More importantly, the fact that you took the initiative to go dive in, build rapport, and understand *their problem* at a deep level makes you look like an A-player in the eyes of a hiring manager. Doing this pre-work alone puts you in the 95% range of consideration. Your competition dam sure isn't putting forth this level of effort, so when you do receive an offer will the feeling of achievement be oh-so-sweet!

It's All About Mindset

There are two critical beliefs that you have to confront when you think about your hunt for employment and the labor market:

1) The job market is flourishing.
2) The job market is lousy.

This is another version of the glass half-full/glass half-empty idea. Which version do you prefer? I personally think it's wiser to be optimistic rather than pessimistic when you prepare your resume and start looking for a job. If you're pessimistic, why even bother? There is a common saying that you have probably heard that says: "Seeing is believing." Well, that's a lie. Believing is actually seeing.

If you *believe* that the job market is getting better, you will have confirmation bias as you are reading the news, Facebook, or any other media outlet. Headlines like the following:

- Hiring is up!
- Company XYZ is planning on hiring 5,000 people
- The unemployment rate is down X%

The opposite can be believed just as easily, but I don't advise it:

- 5,000 people have been laid off at XYZ
- Brand XYZ will be closing dozens of stores
- The unemployment rate is up X%

Isn't that a bit woo-woo? Yeah, but it's certainly better than the alternative.

Chapter 3 Know Your Target

"There is a big difference between graduates who find jobs right away and those who struggle—lack of career focus is the chief reason."[18]

(Image source: Ray Dalio's Principles for Success https://www.youtube.com/watch?v=B9XGUpQZY38)

It's not uncommon for people who have multiple talents and interests to experience difficulty in narrowing focus (I still struggle with this too). So often the approach becomes too broad. As the saying goes, if you chase two rabbits, you won't catch either one. That's a simple way of saying the following:

---

[18] Dr. David DeLong https://www.consumeraffairs.com/news/despite-low-unemployment-many-college-grads-are-out-of-work-061818.html

"If you aren't getting the results you'd like or need from any activity, situation, or relationship, it's probably because your goals are not clearly enough defined, to yourself and to others." – Paul J. Meyer

So often the approach to picking a career is similar to walking up to a random ticket counter in the airport and saying, "Give me a ticket." The agents want to help but are unable to do so unless you give them a destination.[19]

Your target is as essential to your success as air is to life.

Before I discovered the key to success with my resume and the job search, I took the same approach. I would do too many things and try to be self-sufficient in order to save money by doing everything myself and want to feel productive. Well, I'm here to tell you that self-sufficiency is just a way of tricking ourselves. Sure, it shows that we can cover the surface, but that prevents us from going deep into our expertise. Bestselling science writer Matt Ridley puts it this way: *"Self-sufficiency is just another word for poverty."* If I could go back and give this advice to my younger self, I wouldn't hesitate.

The other advice I'd give my younger self is: Specialize in a field much sooner and stick to it. If you haven't picked up on this already, I'm writing this book for the younger version of myself who might be out there. Fortunately, the students I work with not only see results, they also enjoy success in job offers and higher starting salaries.

In his book *Think and Grow Rich,* Napoleon Hill lays out four major causes of career failure, which point to this same

_____

[19] The Magic of Thinking Big by Dr. David Schwartz

problem of trying to be overly self-sufficient. All of these points interconnect with each other:

1) **Undefined life purpose:** *There is no hope of success for the person who does not have a definite purpose, or exact goal, at which to aim.*

2) **Unfitting profession:** *No one can succeed in a job they do not like. The most essential step in marketing yourself is selecting a career into which you can throw yourself wholeheartedly.*

3) **Lacking laser focus:** *The "jack-of-all-trades" is rarely good at any. Concentrate all your efforts on one definite chief aim.*

4) **Poor choice of business partner:** *Select an employer with care who is smart, successful, and inspirational. We subconsciously emulate those with whom we associate most closely. Pick an employer who is worth emulating.*[20]

A sense of belonging becomes very real with repeated rejections or losing a job. Knowing where your next meal is going to show up as you exhaust all of your options can chip away at self-worth and mental wellness. I've encountered this with students from undergrad to grad school. Hill's foresight can help mitigate that. Recent research suggests that passion projects are increasingly going to become more important to the next generation. Meaningful work on a large scale will be more desirable than ever before, so why not try to tap into that

---

[20] Think and Grow Rich by Napoleon Hill

now? Leap from a job into a vocation that becomes a calling. See the graph at the end of this chapter.

> *"Those who take the haphazard approach of an unplanned life will struggle more."*
> - Craig Ballantyne

What do I do first? Which way should I go? Staring into the abyss of your career options can feel daunting.

> "Deciding what <u>not</u> to do is as important as deciding what to do."
> - Steve Jobs

In *The Snowball: Warren Buffett and the Business of Life*, Buffett shares a sage piece of advice to help us cope with this uncertainty:

> *People ask me where they should go to work, and I always tell them to go to work for people whom they admire the most. It's crazy to take little in-between jobs just because they look good on your resume. That's like saving sex for old age. Do what you love and work for whom you admire the most, and you've given yourself the best chance in life you can.*

It's worth wrangling with the following questions to yourself:

1) Imagine for a second that you only had 12 months left to live. What would you do?
2) Who do you look up to? Who are your role models?
3) What brought you joy as a child?
4) As you go about your day what brings you the most happiness?
5) Visualize yourself at 90 years old: What do you want to look back and remember about your life? What regrets would silently break your heart? What do you wish you would have taken action on when you were younger?

Those questions are harder to answer than you thought, right? Famed adventurist and CEO Richard Branson suggests the following approach:[21]

1. What do you love?
Make a list of all the things you are passionate about or that interest you. It doesn't matter how trivial or random the items are, or if they don't appear to lead to an entrepreneurial idea — one could spark an idea that turns into a business.

2. What do you dislike?
Next, think about things that annoy, confuse or even anger you. If you ran the world, what changes would you like to make? Again, do not censor your thoughts: just write!

While the above questions are good primers in helping you think about your skills and interests, getting to your real "why" is what you should strive for. Self-deception or being unwilling to have radical self-honesty with yourself will only create misguided feelings and delay you from tapping into your gifts. Understanding your "why" gets to your sole purpose. The following WHY exercise will help you answer your "why" by going several layers deep.

What is it about _____ that is important to you? The blank area can be your career, a skill you want to learn, or the person you aspire to become (a.k.a. your future self 2.0). Write the first answer that comes to mind.

[21] https://www.virgin.com/richard-branson/tackling-challenges-curiosity

After you fill in the blank, try to answer that question: What is it about _____ that is important to you? When you get an answer, loop it back into the original question, put your answer in the blank, and then try to answer this new question. Take your answer to this question and repeat the process. This will move you to a much deeper understanding of your why.

Here is a sample of what mine looks like:
Q: What is it about writing a book for recent graduates that is important to me?
A: Because I struggled on my own and learned a ton in the process.

Q: What is it about struggling on my own and learning a ton in the process that is important to me?
A: I can vividly remember the pain that came with rejection and not knowing what to do.

Q: What is it about vividly remembering the pain of rejection and not knowing what to do that is important to me?
A: I questioned my self-worth and felt angry at myself for spending so much money on an education that wasn't paying dividends.

You'll want to do the same and go seven to eight layers deep. The first few are easy, and it's usually around layer four or five that a shift from logical to emotional occurs. Being honest in your responses can help reveal your why. Should you actually follow through the line of questioning then don't be surprised if you start to get clarity.

If you need more practical reading on this area, I suggest *The Career Manifesto: Discover Your Calling and Create an Extraordinary Life* by Mike Steib.

After you discover your why you will automatically be in a category that allows you to specialize. Align that specialization to a gap within the market, or an underserved market.

If you think about it, every animal and insect in nature specializes in some way, so why don't we? Often, when starting out in our careers, we don't specialize for fear of boxing ourselves in or leaving money on the table. Instead, even though Napoleon Hill warns against it in his four rules, we decide to be jacks of all trades and masters of none. When you decide to go after several things at once, you end up sacrificing your fccus and your ability to go in-depth.

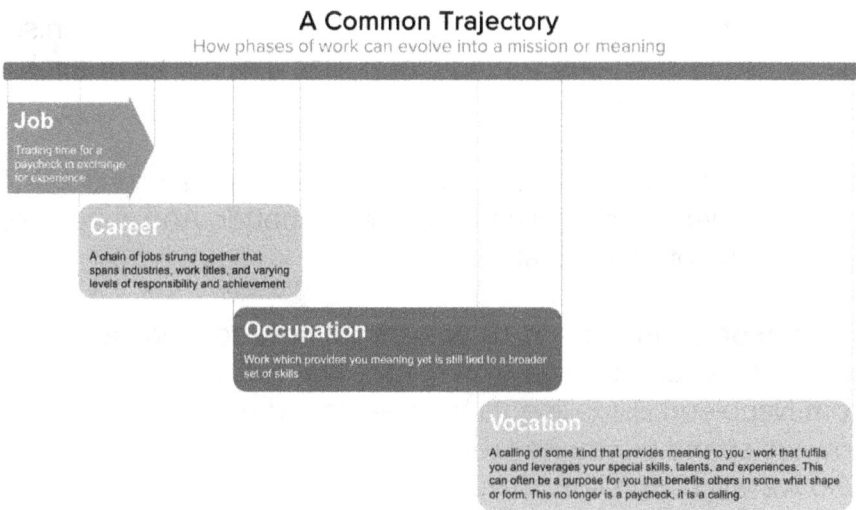

A Common Trajectory
How phases of work can evolve into a mission or meaning

Job
Trading time for a paycheck in exchange for experience

Career
A chain of jobs strung together that spans industries, work titles, and varying levels of responsibility and achievement

Occupation
Work which provides you meaning yet is still tied to a broader set of skills

Vocation
A calling of some kind that provides meaning to you - work that fulfils you and leverages your special skills, talents, and experiences. This can often be a purpose for you that benefits others in some what shape or form. This no longer is a paycheck, it is a calling.

A paycheck is good, but it is temporary. Value and equity compound to build wealth.

A better way to approach this is to look at your career for what you see yourself doing in 10 years. Start with where you're living, your family, your job title, and your social group in 10 years. Then work backwards from there. Consider this:

"As children, all of us set high goals. At a surprisingly young age we made plans to conquer the unknown, to be leaders, to attain positions of high importance, to do exciting and stimulating things, to become wealthy and famous — in short, to be first, biggest, and best. And in our blessed ignorance we saw our way clear to accomplish these goals."[22]

We did it then, as children, and we can do it again here.

Use the four Fs: Family, Friends, Fitness, and Finances to describe in vivid detail where you want to be. Write down on a piece of paper the following:

By this date: _____ ____, 20xx I will be standing… (finish the sentence and keep writing more). Use the four Fs to think about your answer.

Ideally what you write should be three-to-five pages in length. The more detail that you can provide the better. And, whatever you do, do not think small.

The person you will be in 10 years from now depends almost entirely on your future environment.[23] We hear the same advice from Napoleon Hill telling us how we spend our free time, and how we spend our money will determine where we will be and who we will become in 10 years' time.

Your future self is the person you want to be. For myself, I'll sometimes sit and simply visualize in my mind of what my future self is doing, fixate on that, then work backwards from there. For you, the future you 2.0 that you're developing into should be guided by that version of you years down the road.

_____

[22] The Magic of Thinking Big by Dr. David Schwartz
[23] The Magic of Thinking Big by Dr. David Schwartz

For example maybe you currently scroll and click through Facebook, Instagram, or Snap until it's time to see what's on Netflix. Yet, your future you 2.0 is actively working towards your goals and the free time you do have is restoring your attention and being intentional about who you surround yourself with.

"Life is too short to be little" - Benjamin Disraeli

Chapter 4 Riches Are in the Niches

Permit me to share a few quotes that have meant a lot to me during my own employment journey:

"Success demands singleness of purpose" – Vince Lombardi

"The things which are most important don't always scream the loudest. – Bob Hawke

"We are kept from our goal, not by obstacles but by a clear path to a lesser goal."
– Robert Brault

What makes you special is the point of differentiation. That's the purpose to you, and for some people this can take years to understand. The topic of purpose. Setting up incentives to fuel the creation and setting up conditions to create your maximum potential—that's what the world needs from you. What makes you different? How are you different or unique to your friends and family? Your uniqueness is the difference. This is your niche in the economy. One of my favorite educators is E.O. Wilson, who is also the world's leading expert on ants. Wilson is unique because of an accident that he experienced as a young boy. The accident left him with limited scope of vision in one eye that prompted him to focus on "the little things" like ants instead of what other kids his age were doing. That stoked his interest in insects.

Yes, niches even apply to resume books. When looking at resume books online we see a widening approach from resumes of all things to resumes with a very narrow focus like resumes for veterans.

Google

Resumes for

resumes for high school students
resumes for teachers
resumes for college students
resumes for dummies
resumes for customer service
resumes for teenagers
resumes for 2018
resumes for internships
resumes for restaurant
resumes for first job

Google Search   I'm Feeling Lucky

	Book	Rating	# of reviews	Year written
1	Resume for Dummies	4.6	29	2015
2	How to write the perfect resume	4.8	25	2018
3	Ladders 2018 resume guide	4.3	99	2018
4	The resume writing guide	4.9	25	2014
5	Modernize your resume	4.5	12	2016
6	Knock 'em dead resumes	4.4	155	2015
7	The winning resume	3.5	85	2015
8	Resume psychology	4.9	46	2015
9	Resume writing secrets from a corporate recruiter	4.9	10	2018
10	What color is your parachute: rethinking resumes	4.2	37	2014
11	Resume magic: trade secrets	4.1	80	2010
12	The golden resume	4.6	80	2015
13	Resume the definiative guide	4	6	2017
14	Resume ground breaking secrets	3.8	20	2016
15	No mistakes resume	4.6	41	2013
16	Lose the resume land the job	3.7	8	2018
17	F*ck your resume	3.8	58	2016
18	Damn good resume guide	4.3	21	2012
19	Perfect phrases for resumes	3	6	2005
20	Elements of resume style	3.5	6	2014
21	How to write an amazing IT resume	4.5	22	2017
22	Steal this resume 500	3.9	28	2014
23	Resume writing 2018	2.9	22	2016
24	Resume writing for IT professionals	4.3	16	2014
25	RIP resume	4.8	55	2016
26	Signs of a great resume: Veterans edition	5	44	2014
27	Signs of a great resume	4.7	63	2012
28	Resumes that stand out: College students and recen	4.8	50	2014
29	Resume: the secret to writing a resume to guarantee	3.6	16	2016
30	Creating your first resume	5	3	2016

(Image source: Google.com)

Out of the top 30 resume books sold on Amazon, only four narrow their focus to a specific audience. A simple Google autocomplete prompt does what most resume books should do; unfortunately, many resume books fail to carve out a niche and instead create titles that try to serve everyone with outdated information. The four gray highlights above illustrate a narrow focus, which is better because it is specific.

Take, for instance, Olympic athletes. They are often so athletic and well-trained that they are good at many other sports. Swimming and water polo, for example, are similar and complement one another, but it's more difficult to expect someone to be good at, say, ski jumping and sailing, which couldn't be more different. Jacob Tullin Thams, Olympic gold and silver medalist in sailing and ski jumping, this is the exception and not the rule!

Even though this kind of versatility is admired in sports, you don't want to position yourself as being able to do the same thing on your resume. This will create problems not only for the computer scanning software that seeks keywords, but also for the HR reps. When your LinkedIn profiles and resumes aren't focused on a single position or sport, you are essentially shooting yourself in the foot for no good reason. This is a common resume mistake that you are going to want to avoid.

When you associate yourself with too many areas of specialization, each of these connected areas will be undermined rather than if you focus on a single one. Google as a search engine is a good example of this. Even though Google offers an amazing variety of services, they initially started off as a simple search engine and nothing more. Yahoo is tied with being a web portal as well as a search engine, but Google takes the crown for search capability because Yahoo undermines itself by doing too much rather than being laser-focused. Amazon now sells everything, but when first starting out they only sold books.

I don't know about you, but when I was in junior high school I was socially awkward. I didn't know where the hell I fit in or what friends or crowd to associate with (let alone explore groups carefully without risk of standing out too much). Standing out too much would have been a social risk. One part of me at the time didn't care (rebellious streak) and the other part of me just wanted to fit in. I can remember getting into a fist fight after school, and despite our clobbering of one another, my ego and social perception in school weighed far more to me than worrying about my own physical condition. Fitting in is real as a kid, and that same sort of familiar comfort can carry on with us as we mature. As an adult, though, fitting in can only take you so far, which is why differentiation is so critical.

Where can you stand out?

The most difficult part of the resume process for those starting out and those early in their careers is selecting a specific area. You want to get as narrow as possible with your resume to cut through the noise in the marketplace. As simple as that may sound, many people never do this with their resumes. But you're not going to do what these people do (or fail to do), right? Don't be afraid to mess up. Anything worth doing is worth doing poorly at first.

Here's another compelling reason to specialize. Assume for a second that you're playing in differing Olympic sports (or jobs, for that matter) and that you're marketing yourself to HR reps, headhunters, recruiters, and hiring managers. What do you think will happen? It will show them that you aren't a specialist in their sport, their field of interest. They will perceive it as noncommittal and not being an expert in THE area that they're hiring for. That's why trying to please everybody is a losing strategy. Here is the hard reality:

Today's job market belongs to those who specialize.

That's the truth. Not long ago I had a couple of students tell me that they were interested in careers in HR, consumer research, and customer experience. Fantastic! I said, pick one. One student responded with HR. So I asked: What specialized area of HR do you want? My advice to each of them was this: Pick one specific area and then read everything you can get your hands on that deals with that chosen field. Then get a mentor.

HR

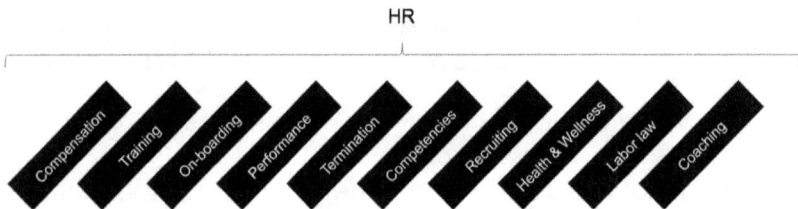

If you're having a tough time deciding what field to enter because you have skills in many opposing areas, that's a sign that you'll need more than one resume, and you will have to make up your mind about what field you want.

Here is another hard reality to consider:

**If you don't pick a career or job field,
someone will do it for you.**

To put it another way: Specializing is like what happens when a company takes one of their generic, mass-produced products, moves it into a niche, and that automatically permits a price increase. The same can be said for you when you specialize. You de-commoditize yourself and your value goes up.

But maybe you're still exploring your options and aren't sure what job or career to choose. That's okay! Exploring is quite common. It's an ordinary part of the job journey. To help you narrow down what you're naturally suited for, I'd suggest the following tools and assessments:

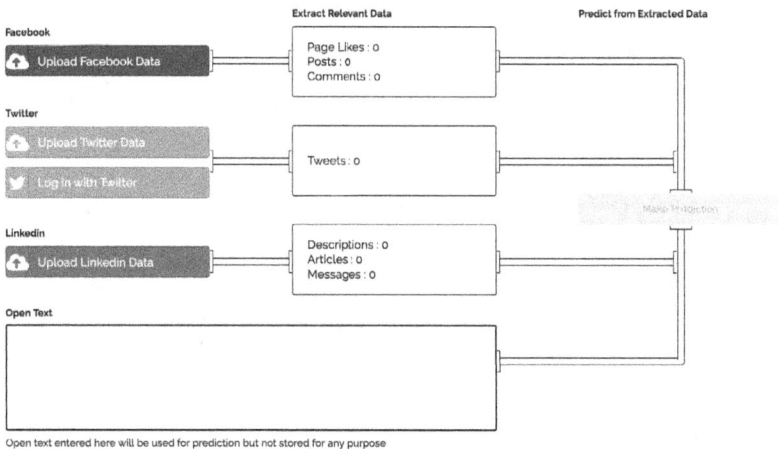

Extract Relevant Data   Predict from Extracted Data

Facebook

⬆ Upload Facebook Data

Page Likes : 0
Posts : 0
Comments : 0

Twitter

⬆ Upload Twitter Data

🐦 Log in with Twitter

Tweets : 0

Linkedin

⬆ Upload Linkedin Data

Descriptions : 0
Articles : 0
Messages : 0

Open Text

Open text entered here will be used for prediction but not stored for any purpose

(Image source: https://applymagicsauce.com)

ApplyMagicSauce - This free tool from the Psychometrics Centre at the University of Cambridge uses your psycho-demographic profile from digital footprints of your behavior. It reveals how you might be perceived by others online and provides academically robust insights on your personality, intelligence, leadership, life satisfaction and more. Every citizen has a right to understand their data, but most big tech companies would rather not reveal what is predictable (or profitable) about you. Fortunately, you can now download your social media data and analyze it directly using their tool.

<u>CliftonStrengths 34</u> - This is by far the most accurate personality assessment on the market from the Gallup organization. As of writing, the fee is $49 yet it is the fastest and most accurate way for you to understand your unique talents. There is even a portion of the report that has "What Makes You Stand Out?" Take note of your results from the report and notice how you emotionally respond while reading it. Be mindful of nervous ticks, body sensations, or emotions. Those signals can be significant clues to understanding your purpose.

<u>PathSource</u> - Another option is this fast and free career assessment for your smartphone.

Focus on what you care about, not what is fun

A Harvard Business School professor recently analyzed every graduation speech given in the last 10 years at the top 100 U.S. universities:

"I plucked out instances where speakers gave students advice on how to pursue their passion. Much of the advice centered on "focusing on what you love" as the way to follow your passion. But some speakers described the pursuit of passion as "focusing on what you care about." The distinction is subtle but meaningful: focusing on what you love associates passion with what you enjoy and what makes you happy, whereas focusing on what you care

about aligns passion with your values and the impact you want to have."[24]

Don't worry if you still do not know your most employable qualities, are simply exploring options, or just want a change because you're tired of what you're currently doing. All of these are normal, acceptable situations that many of us have experienced at least once in our lives. When I was in school (no, we're not going to talk about when that was 😎), it was said that people change their jobs and careers five to seven times in their lifetime. Today, that number has grown to 12 to 15... and job-hopping is no longer stigmatized the way it once was.[25]

Cumulative number of jobs held from ages 18 to 52, by sex and age

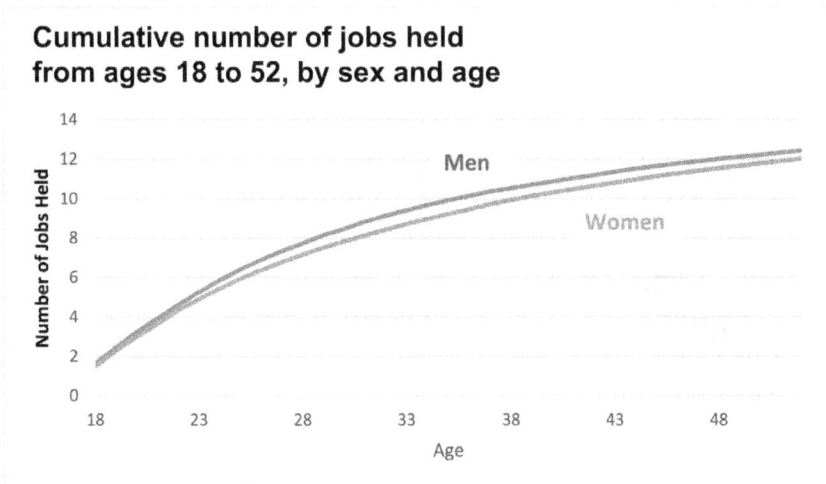

(Image source BLS 2019 https://www.bls.gov/news.release/pdf/nlsoy.pdf)

So much of life is figuring out what you want by adjusting your journey at key growth stages to pivot a few centimeters or several miles towards a path that is better aligned with your values and intentions.

---

[24] https://hbr.org/2019/10/3-reasons-its-so-hard-to-follow-your-passion

[25] https://www.thebalancecareers.com/how-often-do-people-change-jobs-2060467

In short, it all comes down to what you want. If you don't know what you want, then any target goal will do. What type of clothes do you want to be wearing? What kind of people do you want to socialize with? Where do you want to live? Your needs will direct your feelings while influencing your values, and understanding what you need helps put guardrails around your target.

The famous educator Earl Nightingale said that you could make yourself a world-class expert in most fields simply by studying every available resource on the topic for an hour a day for just a year. That's six months with two hours a day. Are you up for the task?

Ok, as a reader you may be thinking of another axiom: If you want to hear God laugh, tell him your plans. If that's the case, why bother? Well, the answer is simple: Imperfect results from a clearly-defined target are still far superior to random results on a whim.

Self-improvement means knowing what to go after, and income improvement follows self-improvement.

"Capitalism rewards things that are both rare and valuable."
-Scott Adams

Ok, enough background information. Let's get into your story!

Chapter 5 Fresh Eyes See What You Cannot

Any well-polished piece of work requires help. This is where your friends and family can help you see your blind spots and aid in helping pull out your narrative.

No need to open your resume on your computer for this. Go and find someone to interview you (ideally for 60 minutes), and record the conversation. You'll be surprised at the small nuggets of gold that can come from this exercise.

Questions for your interviewer to consider asking you:

1) What excites you about what you're currently doing or want to be doing?
2) Describe a time when you were beaming with pride at a job or on a project.
3) Can you tell me about your on-boarding process at your last job… what was that like?
4) What are some things that frustrate you about your current or previous job?
5) What sort of technologies did you work with in school or your past job?
6) Who did you report to for projects?
7) What type of people did you cross-collaborate with in your current or past role?
8) How were you measured in your current or past roles?
9) How would your classmates or colleagues describe you?
10) Were you ever recognized or praised by anyone for your efforts on a class project or in your past job?

The answers to these questions will help create the content for your resume. Either do the work now by answering these questions or pay handsomely to have a resume writer to do it for you. Now let's break down your responses as they apply to your resume.

Chapter 6 The Mechanics

Go and find three job postings for the position that you're after and read all of them. The content from those postings (job responsibilities, skills, and background) will help you figure out what to write as you match up your skills.

Here's the thing: When you use phrases like *pays close attention to detail* or *I have a proven track record* with someone who looks at dozens of resumes every day, such phrases will make a hiring manager think that this job applicant a) used a template b) copy and pasted from Google or c) desires to possess those skills but doesn't actually have them and hopes to convince the reader otherwise. If you do have those skills, great! Try to find another way to convey your attention to detail. Alternative examples: meticulous level of detail, painstaking effort, or diligent in spotting details that others don't. Everyone has a proven track record. Craft your results by saying, you delivered 12 projects on time, consistently came in under budget, or increase sales month over month.

It's a competitive job market, and if a hiring manager can find one small mistake—like an overused cliche—to disqualify you, he or she will. Too often I find that candidates using phrases like *pays close attention to detail* and *has a proven track record* rarely do. In fact, in my experience I find those resumes have more spelling and grammatical errors versus the ones that don't use these phrases. The same applies when pressing candidates on a screening call to describe their proven track record.

The Quality of the Writing

Language is the currency of the mind. – Jack Trout

Business writing is about clarity and persuasion. The main technique is keeping things simple. Simple writing is persuasive. A good argument in five sentences will sway more people than a brilliant argument in a hundred sentences. Don't fight it.

Simple means getting rid of extra words. Don't write, "He was very happy" when you can write "He was happy." You think the word "very" adds something. It doesn't. Prune your sentences.

Your first sentence needs to grab the reader. Go back and read my first sentence to this post. I rewrote it a dozen times. It makes you curious. That's the key.

Write short sentences. Avoid putting multiple thoughts in one sentence. Readers aren't as smart as you'd think.

Learn how brains organize ideas. Readers comprehend "the boy hit the ball" quicker than "the ball was hit by the boy." Both sentences mean the same, but it's easier to imagine the subject (the boy) before the action (the hitting). All brains work that way. (Notice I didn't say, "That is the way all brains work"?) – Scott Adams[26]

---

[26] Adams, Scott https://dilbertblog.typepad.com/the_dilbert_blog/2007/06/the_day_you_bec.html

Watch your mood

It's best to write when you're in a confident mood because you want your resume to speak with authority. Saying things such as *"I was responsible for XYZ"* will make your reader yawn. Instead, replace such statements with an active voice: *"I launched... I led... I organized... I managed... etc..."* All of these grammatical constructions will demonstrate your drive and self-assurance.

> Your resume is a marketing campaign — the time and effort you put in is what you get out. I'll continue to show you how to cut down your time and effort in the following pages.

Don't be passive

In fact, plan to write every part of your resume in the active voice to the best of your ability. What exactly is the active voice? As the example above suggests, it's a style of voice that avoids passivity and demonstrates action. Here is an expanded version of the example from above: *"I managed a team of three... I launched a new social media campaign resulting in [conversion rate]... I created a stealth [product name] that made it out of concept testing and gained executive buy-in."*

We know who the subject is at all times on your resume—it's you. As a result, active voice is what you should go with. It's also implied that you are the subject ("I").

So, *"I managed a team of three"* can be *"Managed a team of three,"* too.

Passive example: *"Sales were increased 32% within two months..."*

With the passive voice no one owns the behavior. Passive voice is great when you don't know who the subject is or the sentence is unimportant. Yet, you're important and you're the subject, so no passive voice. Consider this example from Ann Handley in *Everybody Writes: Your Go-To Guide to Creating Ridiculously Good Content:*

> Passive example: Instagram has become popular among pizzerias, and as a result many photos of people eating pizza *are being posted.*
>
> Active example: Instagram has become popular among pizzerias, and as a result *people are posting* many photos of themselves eating pizza.

Or these:

> Passive: The video was edited by a guy named Jimmy.
>
> Active: A guy named Jimmy edited the video.
>
> Passive: Classical theme music is rarely featured on podcasts.
> Active: Podcasts rarely feature classical theme music.

Do you see the difference? The passive voice is fine to use in many cases, but not on your resume. Your tone is crucial. As a recruiter scans your resume, you want him or her to be struck by a strong, decisive personality. It's all about communicating confidence: That's what the active voice does.

Avoid shorthand

We live in an age of texts and tweets. Everyone seems to be constantly pressed for time, and that can negatively influence how you create your resume, too. Time constraints do not grant you license to use shortcuts or phrases such as:

> *"Drove benefit packages, negotiating multiple options for benefits at a cost reduction of 29 percent."*

It's unclear what "drove benefit packages" is trying to suggest and the role they were in. Ok, it's a decent attempt at a bullet point, but where is the story?

Here is a better example of how to craft your narrative:

> *"I was responsible for the company's benefit package selection process that entailed driving the RFP process with five vendors. I led a collaborative team that negotiated a multi-option benefit package that exceeded our employees' needs while reducing benefit spend by 29 percent."*[27]

---

[27] https://news.microsoft.com/life/storytelling_resume

Does this make sense? By capturing the narrative and quantifying results you can avoid vagueness and open the door for the HR rep or hiring manager to want to know more.

According to the Professional Association of Resume Writers, proper "resume grammar" means using a lot of sentence fragments, implied subjects, and verb-driven sentence structures. Personal pronouns like "I," "he," and "she" and articles like "a," "an," and "the" are used sparingly if at all.[28]

Just as emojis have emerged to make texting communication more expressive with fewer characters, phrases and fragments carry the weight of full sentences in abbreviated forms that will surely violate your MS Word grammar check's sensibilities. Traditional grammar rules still apply. Also, no need to be too formal.

Punctuation: This sentence is a great indication of specialty usage; semi-colons help connect two thoughts within the same sentence, whether it's considered grammatically correct or not. You'll need to develop mastery using colons, commas, and apostrophes as well.

Sentence Length/Fragments: Guidance from the Professional Association of Resume Writers is to try not to exceed 20 words per sentence as complexity increases along with the likelihood of losing your reader's attention —so break it up. Should you find that a sentence takes up three or four lines of text, you're probably better off breaking that up into two sentences. As you proofread, be aware of that dynamic.[29]

---

[28] The Fun & Fundamentals of Resume Writing 2019 by John Suarez
[29] The Fun & Fundamentals of Resume Writing 2019 by John Suarez

Now that you've considered this short list of mistakes to avoid, we're ready to examine the resume tips and practices that truly work. As I mentioned earlier, all of these "secrets" were discovered in the course of my own job search, my students' searches, and reviewing countless resumes as a hiring manager. These are tried and tested… and they work!

Proofreading Hacks

58% of resumes have typos in them[30]
– Laszlo Bock, Senior VP of People Operations, Google

As you look through your resume for typos, spelling mistakes, and grammatical errors, you might consider reading your resume in reverse. Yes, read your resume backwards rather than from top to bottom, left to right. Reading in reverse will cause your brain to slow down and catch mistakes. As your eyes scan over the words in reverse order, your brain will consider each word independently, allowing you to spot errors more easily (tip provided courtesy of Ann Handley, *Everybody Writes*).[31] Even after you've carefully read your resume forward and backward, you still want to get someone to proofread it for you.

If you find your eyes getting tired of staring at the screen and the words on the page then check out www.Grammarly.com or www.Slickwrite.com for additional help with proofreading. For boldness and clarity check out www.hemingwayapp.com
To beef up your headlines use
https://headlines.sharethrough.com

---

[30] The 5 biggest mistakes I see on resumes and how to correct them
https://www.linkedin.com/pulse/20140917045901-24454816-the-5-biggest-mistakes-i-see-on-resumes-and-how-to-correct-them/
[31] Everybody Writes: Your Go-To Guide for Creating Ridiculously Good Content, by Ann Handley

Chapter 7 Resume Format & Style

Is your resume as fun to read as some software licensing agreements?

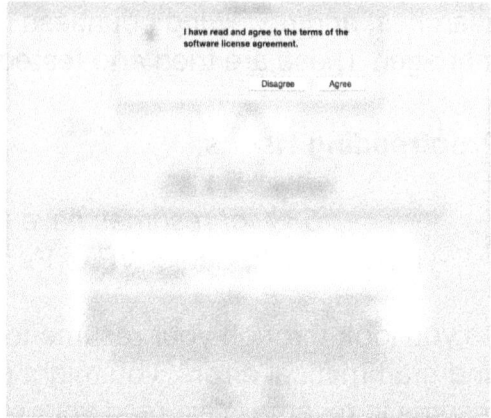

Let's make your resume compelling enough to excite recruiters and HR reps the minute that they read it! That means avoiding some common mistakes. Don't give them an inventory of your skills, and certainly don't give them an exhaustive job history, either.

Recent grads frequently treat their resumes, or LinkedIn profiles, as a comprehensive index of everything they've ever done in the employment world (including that time when they opened a lemonade stand when they were ten years old). All I can say is, hold on. Do you read every page and detail of the user agreement on software updates? I don't, and neither will HR reps. Let's save you (and them) some time by not producing a detailed declaration of your job history and achievements complete with the crayon drawings that you made as a kid.

(Image source: https://www.pinterest.com/pin/250864641716809277)

Here's another example to think about: When we receive yards of paper from a CVS receipt, do we ever read them? Even when those same receipts are blown up into Halloween costumes do we read them? Not likely.

We want to give hiring managers and HR reps the best highlights of your experience to date in a way that creates a powerful narrative that stands above the rest and will lead to an interview. You don't want them to open your resume and find an exhaustive CVS receipt or lengthy user agreement.

Your resume doesn't just market your experience, accomplishments, education, skills, attributes, and qualifications. It brings together all of these components to create a picture of the perceived value you bring to your future employer.

Your Value	Your expertise	Essentially, your value can be viewed as an investment strategy that you're marketing towards. Your future employer is looking to see, out of the candidates available to them, which one is going to give them the best return on their investment (ROI). Again, this is why we want to come out of the gate with a POWERFUL statement that says you can offer them the best ROI.

Your expertise

Your productivity

Your accomplishments

Your education

Your skills

How efficient you are

Your influence

Your reputation

Your qualifications

Your market vision

Essentially, your value can be viewed as an investment strategy that you're marketing towards. Your future employer is looking to see, out of the candidates available to them, which one is going to give them the best return on their investment (ROI). Again, this is why we want to come out of the gate with a POWERFUL statement that says you can offer them the best ROI.

In other words:

You want your resume to communicate that, when they hire you, they're getting a deal. You want them to feel lucky that they found you.

Anyone can create a resume, but very few take the time necessary to cultivate their value in a way that aligns with the job they want. Rather, it's a shotgun approach: copying and pasting information into a Word document, submitting that cut-and-paste resume to dozens of job postings, and hoping for the best. That's a lousy strategy, a waste of time, and it reduces your chances of being credible when you do eventually follow up with a polished version of your resume.

In my experience, there are two types of people who create their own resumes. The first is the person who wants to make sure he or she shines in every possible way by telling you about each and every achievement possible. The second has reservations about bragging and feels that whatever the resume says is just egotistical boasting, and their parents didn't raise them to do that. Some cultures in other countries, like the Netherlands, discourage people from standing out. Neither perspective is right or wrong.

Regardless of which camp you identify with, your options are the same: Attempt to do it yourself or hire someone. This is why people usually pay to have their resumes done by professional resume writers. I've used many of these services myself and very rarely have I used one that produced results or job leads of some kind. I'm sharing my experience with you because, despite how you feel about your qualifications, experience, and education, I believe in you. I am confident that you can not only create a powerful resume that improves your chances of getting callbacks and interviews, but also build on the process of marketing yourself as you grow and go after better-paying positions with more responsibility.

"OK, yes, you're a cow. But you're also a dairy consultant, an expert on calcium, and a hay connoisseur to boot!"

Resume Format & Style

I encourage you to type the word "resume" into Google and then click on the images option to see the multitude of resumes that are out there. Why is that? Well, because there isn't a set standard for resumes. In fact, like people, resumes come in all different colors, shapes, and sizes. The truth is, there's no single format that is correct for your resume.

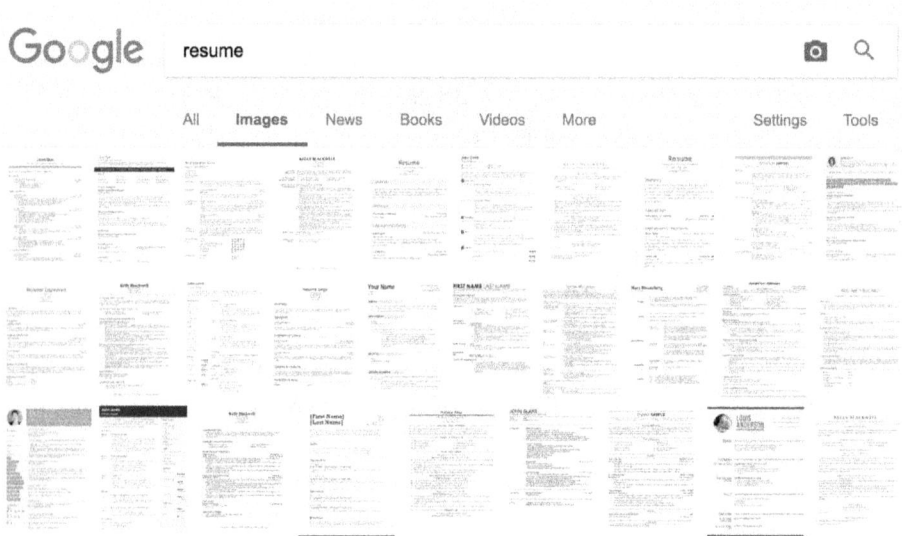

(Image source: Google.com)

This actually creates an advantage for us. With all the different types of resumes and no set standard, how do we know which styles don't work? How do we find the styles that do work? Which resume style should we choose? The options in the above illustration are overwhelming, so I'm going to provide you with some elements from resumes that have been tested by myself and others I've worked with that I know produce results. You'll be able to leverage these elements and strategies for yourself.

How do I know that these work? Because the formats that I'll show you have landed interviews for me, my students, and others. Before I go more into resume style, though, I should first say something about what **not** to include.

A Few Don'ts:

1) Even if you look like Brad Pitt or Angelina Jolie, please don't put your photo on your resume. We have LinkedIn for that. Creative-type roles can get away with this, and you'll see more design elements on their resumes. But business- and corporate-related roles do not need your photo or design elements. 76% of hiring managers automatically reject resumes that include pictures of the applicants.[32]

Vs.

(Image source: Bitmoji)

Katie Burke, chief people officer of HubSpot, says she doesn't want recruiters to see photos during the earliest screening stages. "Photos belong on your personal social-media accounts and online-dating profiles, not your résumé," she says. "What you look like has zero impact on what you can do in a role, so photos, bitmojis and other gimmicks often detract

---

[32] https://www.salary.com/chronicles/9-reasons-your-resume-gets-rejected/

from someone's candidacy versus adding to it."[33]

2) If you're an artist, graphic designer, or wizard at MS Word and can format docs to do things unimaginable, please do NOT put graphics, icons, or images on your resume for business or corporate roles. Save that for your portfolio or personal website.

3) Save the specialized design fonts and colors for your portfolio. I'm a fan of design fonts, but what happens if the hiring manager doesn't have the design font installed on his or her computer? What will your resume look like? Please don't ignore this because often the computer doesn't have instructions to read your design fonts and will default into something crazy that's annoying and unreadable, and that will hurt your chances even more.

What you see	What the manager might see
Designer font: Futura PT	**The computer might display this**
Designer font: Proxima Nova	Τηε χομπυτερ μιγητ δισπλαψ τηισ

As a result, stick with fonts that you know are universal and used across computers. The fonts to stick with are: Arial, Verdana, Times New Roman, or Helvetica. To guarantee readability, I'd advise using Arial, and only Arial.

---

[33] https://www.wsj.com/articles/resumes-are-starting-to-look-like-instagramand-sometimes-even-tinder-11565707364

Proven resume style that lands interviews

The first thing that you might notice is the overall layout. Your resume structure is critical if you want readers to treat it with any depth. You'll also notice that I am not presenting a bunch of resume layouts. Why is that? Well, because this layout has been tested and proven against several others and, when stripped down, this layout has encouraged readership and gets past the electronic resume filters—the two biggest barriers to getting your resume to the next stage, which is the hiring manager's inbox. Are there other layouts that are prettier and well-designed? Of course there are, but good luck getting past the filters. You may already have a structure that works for you, but it may not be delivering the results you want. Pull what you can from the technology and strategies I share with you here to make your resume stand out.

Hey! This is not what career services told me

Resume evolution from the Professional Association of Resume Writers & Career Coaches (PARWCC):

> ...many resumes grew out of the traditional reverse chronological format, meaning they will start with the most recent employment and work backward from there. From a reader's point of view, this is by far the most desirable format and aligns closely with the job application...which is where a lot of the confusion comes from. The "application" mentality is deeply embedded in college career counselors.
>
> Functional resumes used to be considered a strong alternative, but nowadays the functional format is considered undesirable from both your human and computer audiences. The basis of this format was to highlight specific sets of skills instead of employment chronology, and simply listing a job history at the bottom.
>
> What has emerged as a useful alternative is a hybrid resume that combines features of both the chronological and functional formats. More specifically, the chronological framework stays intact with functional components woven into the framework.[34]

The tested format that I'll be sharing with you here is the hybrid format. But what about all those side jobs you had? Shouldn't you list everything? The answer to that is no. Just because a job is omitted from your resume doesn't mean it never happened; it can be left off your resume because it's not the

---

[34] The Fun & Fundamentals of Resume Writing 2019 by John Suarez

most relevant and the amount of real estate you have to work with is limited.

Three Resume Formats: Creative, Business, and LinkedIn's

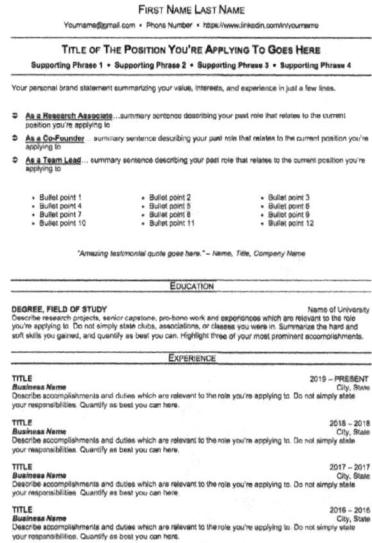

(Image source: https://www.freepik/free-vector/abstract-curriculum-template-with-colorful-waves_1242595.htm - Designed by Freepik)

Creative Resume Style

For:
- Creative agencies
- Advertising firms
- Company cultures that you're 100% sure are creative and prefer this style of resume

Business Resume Style

For:
- Consulting firms
- Fortune 500 companies
- If you're uncertain about the company culture

LinkedIn has started giving recruiters and hiring managers the option to boil down a candidate's LinkedIn profile into small, digestible chunks as the following illustration shows.

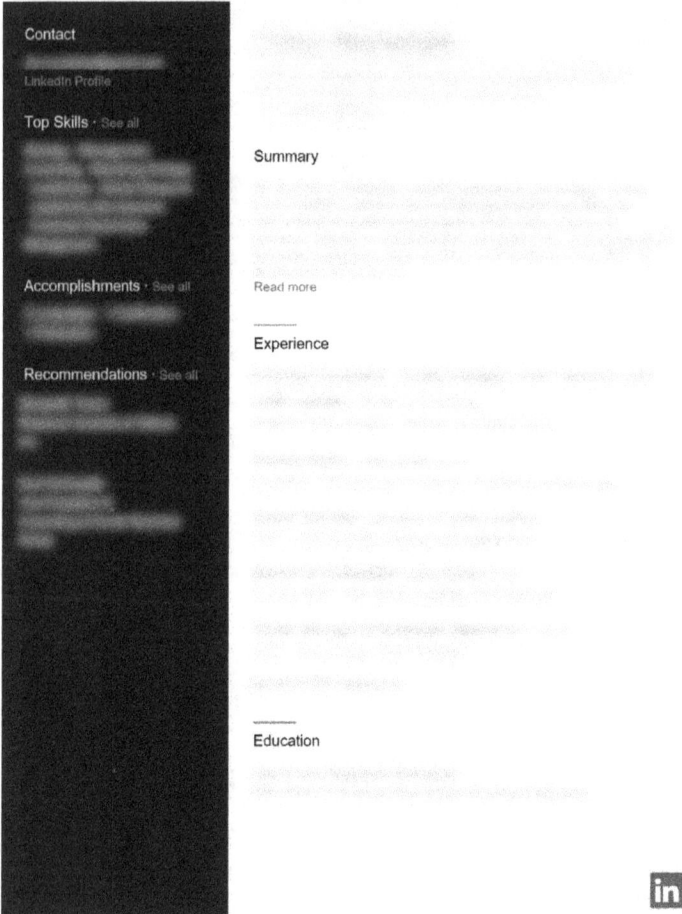

LinkedIn's strategy is to break down a candidate's information into core areas. And, with the use of eye tracking and click stream data, we know that there are critical areas that hiring managers focus on, as well as areas that only a machine filter will pick up.

Interestingly enough, anecdotal data suggests that when looking back at how candidates progress through the stages from phone screening to having an offer made, there are some key themes which can be expected: meets or exceeds experience and interviews well. Yet one that is unexpected is that candidates who advanced to interviews and job offers had similar resume structures like LinkedIn's or the Business resume style.

See examples below:

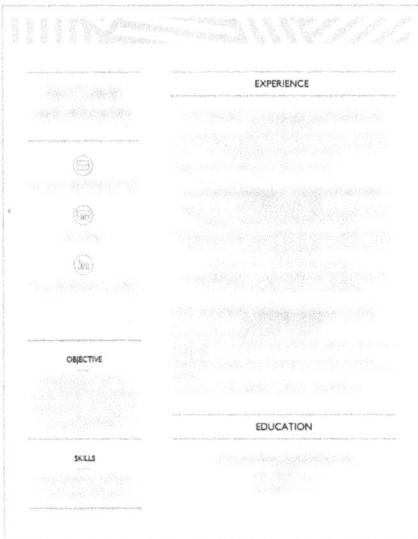

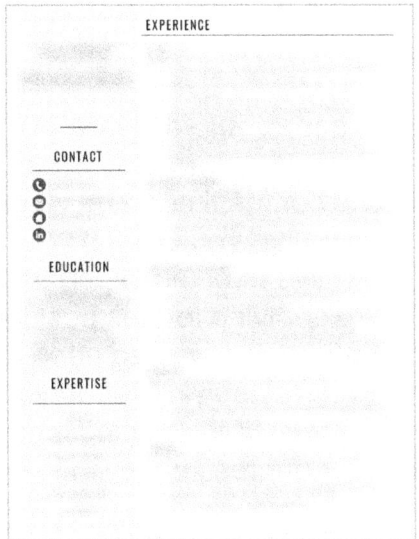

Chapter 8 Why the Top Third is Critical

<u>Your top third is the most important real estate on your resume.</u> Period. Please go back and reread that sentence. In Western culture, with any document or webpage, our eyes naturally start in the upper left-hand corner and scan across to the right. If this section doesn't provide stimulating value in seconds, then we've lost them. Game over.

Even though all of your resume is important, you should focus most of your time on the top third. Assume that the rest of your resume will not be read beyond the top third. Don't hold back. Be aspirational about what you want, explain why you're qualified, and provide an example from the job posting that aligns with your experience.

Be clear about your goal

This is not the time to be vague. I realize you may not know exactly what you want in your career and that's okay! You don't have to be an expert in a field before starting out. But you're applying for this position for a reason. To make sure that this isn't a wasted effort, put the actual job title/position that you're applying for on your resume. Remember: We are not interested in creating a one-size-fits-all resume. We need to tailor our resume, even in small ways, to address specific job openings.

When you do this, it isn't lying: It's aspirational. I cannot emphasize this enough. When you create your resume, you have to check any limiting beliefs you may be harboring about yourself. You'll be able to speak to your actual abilities and highlight your past titles and experiences during the interview.

Remember: This is a marketing campaign, not a time to be humble and modest.

Mailing address: Yes or no?

You may notice that in the resume template illustration below for John Doe there is a spot for the mailing address. Since we no longer live in the age of solely communicating by physical mail, there's no need to list your mailing address. Don't list it. Again, you want to maximize space and get to the point of illustrating your value. Putting your mailing address will eat up space and take away from that. Not including your mailing address is beneficial in another way: You can limit personal identifiers such as address to prevent identity theft.

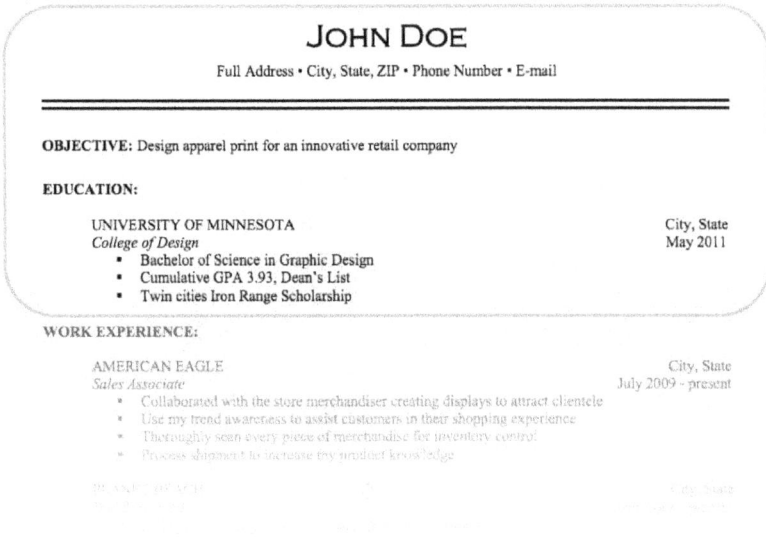

JOHN DOE

Full Address • City, State, ZIP • Phone Number • E-mail

OBJECTIVE: Design apparel print for an innovative retail company

EDUCATION:

UNIVERSITY OF MINNESOTA — City, State
College of Design — May 2011
- Bachelor of Science in Graphic Design
- Cumulative GPA 3.93, Dean's List
- Twin cities Iron Range Scholarship

WORK EXPERIENCE:

AMERICAN EAGLE — City, State
Sales Associate — July 2009 - present
- Collaborated with the store merchandiser creating displays to attract clientele
- Use my trend awareness to assist customers in their shopping experience
- Thoroughly scan every piece of merchandise for inventory control
- Process shipment to increase my product knowledge

(Image source: https://en.wikipedia.org/wiki/File:Resume.pdf)

Can your address hurt your chances?

What about geographical discrimination? If you decide to keep your physical address at the top of the resume, will this hurt your chances? While that can certainly be a factor for some hiring managers in entry-level positions, it's not a hard-and-fast rule. Recruiters of mid-level and executive roles have preferences for their candidates. If they're truly interested in a candidate, companies will ask a candidate to relocate. Only in entry- and mid-level roles will hiring managers have a stronger bias that candidates should be relatively near the office location where they'll be working. Yet, even this is changing as more and more companies become flexible on working remotely.

According to a recruiter friend at a Fortune 100 company (who asked to be kept anonymous), one's location can be a tricky, decisive factor:

> *For example, if a candidate was looking to move to Atlanta, but they're not there yet, then it's advised to list the city and state or greater metropolitan area like "Greater Atlanta Area." Lots of roles do not provide relocation support so that can disqualify a candidate even if they're willing to relocate. The recruiter doesn't know the applicant's plan unless they say so in their resume or during the first phone screening or interview. It can often disqualify them.*

If you're already local to the role and have been for some time, your previous experience can also demonstrate that by listing the city along with the role. The same applies if you're fresh out of school.

To improve your chances of landing an interview, you'll want to open up your geographical preferences rather than simply looking for what's available locally to you.

Top lines: Name, etc.

The first line of your resume is your name. The second line is your email address, followed by your home or cell phone number, and finally your LinkedIn address. I've also seen artists and designers successfully use their Instagram accounts here rather than LinkedIn. I don't suggest sharing your Twitter handle or your Facebook account. Unless you're applying to those specific companies it's best to leave them out.

FIRST NAME LAST NAME

Firstname.Lastname@gmail.com • (234) 567-8910 • www.linkedin.com/in/yourname

TITLE OF THE POSITION YOU'RE APPLYING TO GOES HERE

Supporting Phrase 1 • Supporting Phrase 2 • Supporting Phrase 3 • Supporting Phrase 4

Notice how the LinkedIn address isn't hyperlinked to a blue color with an underline. You'll want to embed the blue hyperlink on a PDF format to make it easy for a hiring manager to click on your profile or portfolio once they're looking at your PDF.

Also notice how the font in the third line is bold and stands out from the rest. What else might you notice? The title you put down is going to be larger in font than your name. I get it. We all want our names to be the most important and the largest piece on our resumes, yet your name is secondary to the title you want. If the HR rep or hiring manager doesn't see what they're looking for in the title, then your name is irrelevant. You want to make your title slightly larger in font and bold so you purposely stand out here. The following illustration shows the common mistake of using a type size that's too large for one's name.

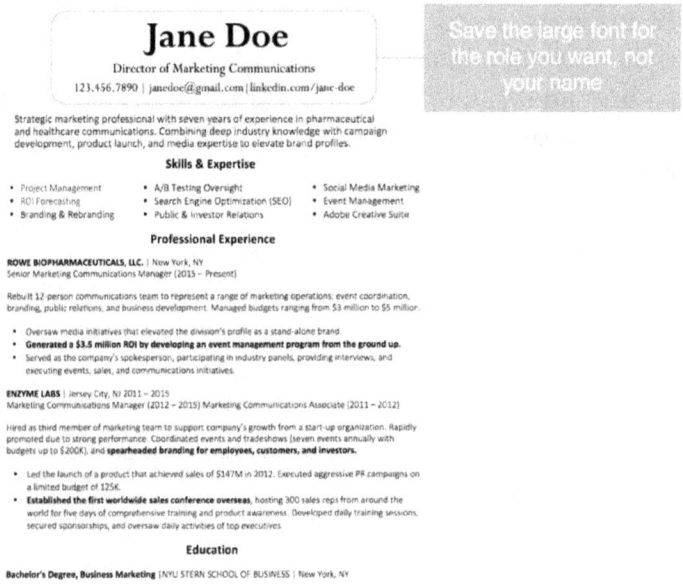

Jane Doe
Director of Marketing Communications
123.456.7890 | janedoe@gmail.com | linkedin.com/jane-doe

Save the large font for the role you want, not your name

Strategic marketing professional with seven years of experience in pharmaceutical and healthcare communications. Combining deep industry knowledge with campaign development, product launch, and media expertise to elevate brand profiles.

Skills & Expertise

- Project Management
- ROI Forecasting
- Branding & Rebranding
- A/B Testing Oversight
- Search Engine Optimization (SEO)
- Public & Investor Relations
- Social Media Marketing
- Event Management
- Adobe Creative Suite

Professional Experience

ROWE BIOPHARMACEUTICALS, LLC. | New York, NY
Senior Marketing Communications Manager (2015 – Present)

Rebuilt 12-person communications team to represent a range of marketing operations: event coordination, branding, public relations, and business development. Managed budgets ranging from $3 million to $5 million.

- Oversaw media initiatives that elevated the division's profile as a stand-alone brand.
- **Generated a $3.5 million ROI by developing an event management program from the ground up.**
- Served as the company's spokesperson, participating in industry panels, providing interviews, and executing events, sales, and communications initiatives.

ENZYME LABS | Jersey City, NJ 2011 – 2015
Marketing Communications Manager (2012 – 2015) Marketing Communications Associate (2011 – 2012)

Hired as third member of marketing team to support company's growth from a start-up organization. Rapidly promoted due to strong performance. Coordinated events and tradeshows (seven events annually with budgets up to $200K), and **spearheaded branding for employees, customers, and investors.**

- Led the launch of a product that achieved sales of $147M in 2012. Executed aggressive PR campaigns on a limited budget of 125K.
- **Established the first worldwide sales conference overseas,** hosting 300 sales reps from around the world for five days of comprehensive training and product awareness. Developed daily training sessions, secured sponsorships, and oversaw daily activities of top executives.

Education

Bachelor's Degree, Business Marketing | NYU STERN SCHOOL OF BUSINESS | New York, NY

Too big: This resume writer is overemphasizing her name and understating the job that she wants. (Image source: https://imagesvc.timeincapp.com/v3/mm/image)

You want to clearly communicate the title of the job that you want. It doesn't matter that you don't have the title in your work experience. This statement is aspirational, and the sub-phrases underneath will support that aspiration. These supporting phrases are the skills that you have or descriptions of your relevant past successes. Examples of these include statements such as: I drove customer satisfaction scores, I hired and managed a team of agile developers, I mentored new employees, I achieved sales revenue of $— … you get the idea.

Email that's stale

Regarding the best email account to list on your resume, the answer should be obvious, but in case it's not, here it is: If you don't have a professional-looking email with gmail.com, me.com, or fastmail.com, then you're going to need to get one.

Keep the address simple and professional with: your first name dot last name. Refrain from using numbers within your email name. Don't use the year that you were born to control for age discrimination and identity theft. With emails that have more than two numbers, filtering software may interpret the email as a spammer tracking code. If you need to, use www.namechk.com and www.gmailavailability.com to search for a username that isn't already taken.

What if you still have your school's email address? I realize that many are proud of the brand and prestige that can come from a well-branded university, but for hiring managers it's irrelevant unless you know for a fact that they are alumni from your school. Commonality sometimes helps build rapport.

If not, then it's a safe bet to go with a modern email address from the free providers I mentioned above. I don't recommend Yahoo, AOL, or Outlook/Hotmail. These are regarded by many as stale, and you don't want a hiring manager to associate your name with being outdated.

Fonts, other settings for the top of the resume

First line --→	FIRST NAME LAST NAME
Second line --------------------→	Firstname.Lastname@gmail.com • (234) 567-8910 • www.linkedin.com/in/yourname
Third line ------------------→	TITLE OF THE POSITION YOU'RE APPLYING TO GOES HERE
Forth line ------------→	Supporting Phrase 1 • Supporting Phrase 2 • Supporting Phrase 3 • Supporting Phrase 4

In regards to mixing and matching fonts, the professional association of resume writers suggests that some *"fonts look very sharp at 8-pt or 10-pt, but not so much at 12-pt or 16-pt...and vice versa. While it is not advisable to use several different fonts throughout the document, it is not uncommon to use one font for the body text and another for your section headings or drop caps to give off the look of customized letterhead. Keep fonts between 10-12-pt for text and 14-20-pt for headings. Don't be afraid to mix and match fonts if you think one looks better as a heading, or vice versa. Limit your presentation to no more than two different font choices."* [35]

The basic rule is just to be consistent in your use of drop caps, italics, boldface, or underline.

Making a statement

At the top of your resume, lines five through nine are of critical importance. This is an area where you want to focus your efforts and make every word count. If you can present your brand statement here in just one line, then you should do it. You don't want to put misleading fluff or filler here. That's a no-no. You want to be as precise as possible. That conveys to the HR rep and hiring manager that you understand the role, can do the job, and can beat out the competition who are applying for the same position.

---

[35] The Fun & Fundamentals of Resume Writing 2019 by John Suarez

Lines 5-9

Onboarding architect, cultural change agent, HR healthcare business partner who blends the humanistic needs of employees and the business needs of the organization by measuring moments that matter, inspiring change, and reducing cost. Maintains a growth mindset with constant learning and continuous self-improvement.
Optional line 8
Optional line 9

If you've ever seen heat maps of eye-tracking software (like the following illustration), then you may realize the importance of the top third, specifically lines five through nine, of your resume and why you must carefully arrange the content there.

How do you know what to write in lines five through nine for your tagline/personal branding statement?

There's no need to feel overwhelmed. I often hear from new graduates who say they don't think that they have much experience in the field in which they are applying. That's okay! You can state what kind of expert you want to become and why you've identified this role and company to be the best at what they do.

(Image source: Ladders report: Keeping an eye on recruiter behavior
https://cdn.theladders.net/static/images/basicSite/pdfs/TheLadders-EyeTracking-StudyC2.pdf)

Do this even if you have to demonstrate your effort. List conferences that you've attended, books that you've read, and blogs or papers that you've published that are relevant to the role you're seeking. You can even include people you've interviewed about the role. Your brand statement might say something like this:

> I've been so fascinated about [this topic] from the time that a guest speaker came to my classroom when I was a student at X Univeristy. I've since read the top 20 books on Amazon about the topic, I've attended [industry conference], interviewed CEOs from [such and such firms], and written extensively on the topic. While I've been told that I'm ahead of my peers in knowing about [the topic] I realize that I still have a lot to learn and I'm thirsty for more. Based upon [company's thought leadership] I'd love the opportunity to be able to contribute.

This kind of statement is sure to grab the attention of an HR rep or a hiring manager. Why? A statement like that is dripping with ambition.

Another way to write your brand statement is to list your values. If you've taken the CliftonStrengths 34 mentioned in chapter 3, that will be an easy task. If you haven't, I'd recommend it. Another option is to sit down with your family and friends to help you craft what they think are your strongest skills in addition to what your values are. How do you find your values? Easy. What are the things that make you really angry? These are the items that violate your values. If you find that your values happen to align with the company where you're applying, then it's worth including that within your personal statement.

If you're still struggling to come up with your personal statement, I'd advise going to two places, LinkedIn and CoMatch, to find professionals working in the role you want. I'd recommend looking at a minimum of 12 profiles as that will provide you with a small but good dataset of examples. Be mindful that your profile will show up on their LinkedIn. Maybe you want people to know that you're looking at their profiles, but if you don't, then you'll need to set your profile to view anonymously.

You can adjust this at: https://www.linkedin.com/psettings/profile-visibility.

Search for the industry and the role that you're interested in. The profile statements will help give you an idea of how experts or less-experienced professionals are positioning themselves in their field. It will also allow you to reach out for potential mentoring and, more important, how you can differentiate yourself from the pack. Seek out seasoned professionals in their field who are often sought after for their opinion to help solve a particular problem. More often than not they will be authors and speakers, just like yours truly.

I don't want you to simply go copy their headlines into your personal statement. I want you to look at the people who are already doing what you want to be doing, then you can reverse-engineer their approach. Copy their way of thinking, their marketing, not their descriptions. Carefully look at how they are trying to be perceived by the audience shopping for them. Depending upon the industry, the professionals you view and their education and training may not be replicable to you because it could be dated, and that's totally fine. That gives you an angle for approaching them and asking them how they would approach their role today if they had to do it all over again.

Really dedicate yourself to spending time on crafting your personal statement. Feel free to read ahead in this book, but, until your personal statement is refined, you'll need to come back to it.

If you are unclear about your personal statement and your goal, I can promise you that the hiring manager will be unclear about responding.

Below are a couple of profile summary examples provided by LinkedIn:

Jess is a professional, hard-working, and detail-oriented virtual marketing and executive assistant with a track record of accomplishment both academically and as an employee. She is the proud Director of Calm at Don't Panic Management, the first virtual assistant agency to embody a people-first approach to virtual assistant success. Since 2011, she's been making matches between chaotic, overworked entrepreneurs and focused, calm virtual assistants. Don't Panic's services include social media marketing, content management, scheduling and booking appointments, travel arrangements, research, data entry, email marketing, WordPress management, editorial management, invoicing and bookkeeping, project management, event planning, and much more. Jess is always open to partnering with dynamic companies and teams who need virtual assistance on a deeper level. Contact hello@dontpanicmgmt.com or visit http://dontpanicmgmt.com for more information.

Specialties: virtual assistance, bookkeeping, travel arrangements, scheduling, social media, account management, online advertising, event planning, digital marketing, consulting, wordpress, mailchimp, convertkit, content management, copywriting, customer relations, market research, marketing, meeting facilitation, microsoft office, Google Suite, newsletters, proposal writing, public speaking, writing

Brian Fanzo is a millennial keynote speaker who inspires, motivates, and educates businesses on how to leverage emerging technologies and digital marketing – to stand out from the noise and engage with customers of all ages. https://www.brianfanzo.com

He has a diverse background working for the Department of Defense in cybersecurity, then as a technology evangelist at a booming cloud computing startup. He is currently the Founder of ISocialFanz, which has helped launch digital and influencer strategies with the world's most iconic brands like Dell, EMC, Adobe, IBM, UFC, Applebees, and SAP.

Brian's #ThinkLikeAFan philosophy has powered first-of-their-kind storytelling campaigns for many Fortune 50 enterprise companies and his upcoming book Press The Damn Button takes that experience to the next level providing a gameplan for telling authentic stories powered by technology to standout from today's digital noise.

A proud pager-wearing millennial and dad of three girls, he hosts three podcasts (FOMOFanz, Just Try This & SMACtalk), has traveled to over 74 countries, and has spoken at many of the world's largest events including South By Southwest, Social Media Marketing World, Consumer Electronics Show, and Mobile World Congress.

He is also a diehard Pittsburgh sports fan, and a semi-professional poker player that isn't afraid to leverage his fast-talking skills to read your body language and spot when you're bluffing!

(Image source: https://business.linkedin.com/marketing-solutions/blog/best-practices--thought-leadership/2018/add-punch-to-your-linkedin-profile-using-these-examples-as-inspi)

Chapter 9 Reinforce with Targeted Bullet Points

⊃ **As a Digital Manager**...identified new sales territories and within 9 months the sales team was performing at an increase of 129% from the previous year's sales

⊃ **As a Finance Manager**...worked with our IT team to validate new system data and caught a significant error that would have resulted in small overpayments resulting in $120k of savings

⊃ **As a Digital Sales Manager**...established a process within our delinquent client portfolio to reduce our delinquency ratio of accounts from 20% to 4% in under 12 months, which beat out our lead competitor

Targeted bullet points come to us from the world of copywriting. There are many different types of bullet points, but we are focusing on targeted bullet points that consist of a short one- or two-sentence statement indicated by the symbol of a dot, checkmark, or circle that highlights each of your biggest achievements.

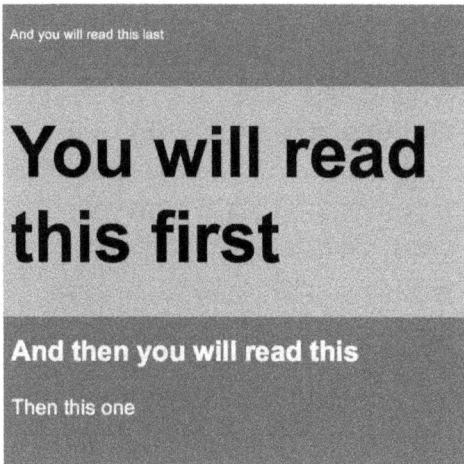
And you will read this last

You will read this first

And then you will read this

Then this one

Why bother with targeted bullet points if you're going to explain your experience in the lower part of your resume? Because we're smart humans and we rarely, if ever, read a document all the way through the first time. We skim and scan with our eyes. To draw our reader in, we'll want to use these effective targeted bullet points to jar the eye and have our reader stop skimming.

(Image source: https://me.me/i/and-you-will-read-this-last-you-will-read-this-7e18c968f5b94cd5ad77d2a060cc7dd7)

It's the same reason we catch ourselves reading silly headlines while checking out at the grocery store or clicking on that clickbait article from *BuzzFeed* because you want to find out what potato chip flavor you might be.[36]

You'll want to change up the style of bullet points throughout your resume. Don't simply default to the small black circle or the hollow circle bullet point.

Here are a few examples:

➡ ⇨ ⇢ ⇒ • ○ ▶ ▷ ✓ ➤ > ❭ ☑

Beyond the examples provided, don't get too creative with your bullets. Keep them simple.

To duplicate the above arrow example, you'll have a chance to use the font you've always wanted to use: Wingdings. Like the other text sizes, I would recommend size nine for your targeted bullet points. On Macs, you'll find this under the Emoji & Symbols Viewer. Under arrows, there will be an assortment of arrow bullets. Scroll down until you find "Circled heavy white rightwards arrow." Below that you will find a subcategory of arrows listed. Select "Menlo Regular."

The actual content of your targeted bullet point will depend on the biggest accomplishment that you had in the role being highlighted. Stating what you were responsible for will not motivate or inspire. Instead, **focus on the results** of your accomplishment. What was measurable about the results that you achieved? Reduced cost, increased sales, optimized click-throughs, drove conversions, etc.

---

[36] https://www.buzzfeed.com/sarahaspler/what-potato-chip-flavor-matches-your-personality

An even more effective way to use a bullet point is to state losses that were taking place and what you did to resolve them. Thanks to behavioral psychology and the work of Richard Thaler, we know that *"...framing in terms of losses is more effective than simply stating information. The losses nudges the reader in the right direction. People avoid losses far more actively than they seek gains."*

We see this same type of language from companies looking to shift behavior in their customers. In the book *Decoded*, one such company found that when they communicated savings in terms of sales or discounts of $200 a year, there was very little impact. However, when shifting the language to potentially losing $200 a year, they produced a significant response.

Key point: Avoiding a loss and communicating that on a resume will impress a hiring manager more than stating an improvement of XYZ. Now let's build upon that idea by layering in some key phrases to really tailor your message.

Chapter 10 Your Structure

A Few Words about Margins

Do not use a friend's templates and don't use the resume template built into Microsoft Word. Formatting issues from computer to computer can cause your resume to display incorrectly. Instead, create a new 8.5 x 11 Word document and set your margins (top, bottom, left, and right) to one inch. Or you can also go online to this book's website www.ResumeSecretsBook.com and purchase the official tested template where the structure is already set for you and ready to be filled in by you.

You really want to pay attention to your margins here. It has been documented that the wider the width of your resume, the more difficult it is to read. We don't want to wear out the hiring manager's eyes! Stick to one-inch margins all around and, if you absolutely have no choice because you're short on content, narrow the margins to increase readability. See the following line length example. 40 character lines are much more appealing to read than 75 character lines.

"Wandering minds punch holes in comprehension."
- Daniel Goleman [37]

---

[37] Focus: The Hidden Driver of Excellence by Daniel Goleman

Line Length

40 characters

sit essit velit, experum que non pa verspiet faccabo rendusant odit aut quas aut ide vendeli taeped minctus quam ipsam quam et ullis ipsant millaccum aut labori doluptat est, velit landande nulluptatur sinimi, qui volendi net Ehent plam videl ipid quiatium eum, sinvendae. Et verio ideremque volorrum harum, tetur serem int fuga. Et vide a consece rovitior adit atecum acestrum evention restotat. Olor aliquo omnima simus. Uditas doloritium, alicipsandi volupiet ipis in nus acias voluptiam, omnis parum aute corios olor barron omnis webster.

75 characters

Cius mod mod est que molor moditios doluptiis destion et que que nonsendam, nectoreperro il inus molorum qui dolorias aut molo milit, sundici lore, officiae volupta spicto molorrovit, venecer enducip icidemo dem ea et fugitum porit, evelita sintus, odit molore peria derum cum quid eum et pa quaternolorae acilicime porendipsant ut quod quiduciunt occae doluptatur, sus a dusandam quatur sus re sin prerorum elloreperis dolupicias secto cone rem facidus nonsequiati tem quam dolorep erfero experum neceat. Ullaut rent, vit ex est volorecation pla soluptur sam il ilibus voluptatisin re consed quia quiandi ut quis nones quos debis archillam doluptas quidiat. Rio. Ximet, esti dolupid es que dest, qui sum sequias mi, odi cus, iundioriatum corepudae dolorem rem aut prae nos amus, tem quature stiassinist ommodit mintio beres dempel intemol upturn, alicae erfernam dolesci nisqui cus.

Narrower **columns are read more quickly**   Wider **columns are read more slowly**

(Source: https://en.wikipedia.org/wiki/Line_lengt)

Testing the Resume Structure

Using a before and after example of a resume can help us see how effective some of these design elements and guidelines are when put to the test. Blurring out personal identifiers and randomizing the placement of each resume across the sample of participants allowed us to be confident in the strategy.

Q: *Assuming you were the hiring manager trying to fill a role for an internal organizational consultant, which applicant would you call for an interview?*

Resume A

○

Purpose: To consult Fortune 500 companies involving the effective management of human capital. Specializing in organizational and program redesigns, data analysis, and project management.

Professional Experience

Evaluated the organizational culture and developed content for website and social-media recruiting. Developed and delivered training regarding effective interviewing skills for hiring managers. Redesign of onboarding program.

Conducted qualitative and quantitative research to provide evidence-based recommendations regarding employee engagement and performance management for this global organization.

Participated in a 3-day workshop in Change Acceleration Process with managers from varying depts. Observed a union election for technicians.

Performed quantitative and qualitative data collection utilizing surveys. Provided analysis of consumer perceptions regarding brand image and presented data to client.

Automobile re-sale business of auctioned Toyota and Honda vehicles.	2011-2012
TD Ameritrade – Managed personal pattern day-trade stock account – 30% Growth.	2009-2010

Education

Concentration in Organizational / Consumer Psychology

The National Society of Leadership and Success Honors Society / Golden Key International Honor Society

Skills
Strong Communication, Presentation and Facilitation Skills | Microsoft Word, Excel, PowerPoint | SPSS | Survey Design | Quantitative and Qualitative Data Analysis | Research | Leadership | Networking | Collaborating | Project Management | Ethical

Resume B

○

ORGANIZATIONAL CHANGE MANAGEMENT CONSULTANT
Workshop Facilitation • Project Management • Instructional Design • Performance Objectives

Onboarding architect, cultural change agent, HR healthcare business partner who blends the humanistic needs of employees and the business needs of the organization by measuring moments that matter, inspiring change, and reduced cost. Maintains a growth mindset with constant learning and continuous self-improvement.

- ○
- ○
- ○

• Facilitate Trainings	• Front-line Implementation	• Staff Development
• Optimize Processes	• Data-driven Research	• Medical Regulatory & HIPPA
• Build Org Capacity	• Root Cause Analysis	• Design Workshops
• Engage Employees	• Team Building & Leadership	• Voice of the Employee

---

EXPERIENCE

Revitalizing new employee on-boarding as identified through research to be a key touch point within the overall employee experience. Created closed-end employee listening through on-going surveys and in-person interviews to gauge motivation and address employee pleasantness pay roll. Keeping a pulse on culture through quantitative and qualitative surveys. Developed new content for our online and social media recruitment campaigns. Facilitate training to management on new compliance and best practices.

Oversaw and provided guidance to a short-term change acceleration process. Engaged with managers from varying depts. Gained an understanding of how change management frameworks were being applied in real-time.

Managed a 6-month organizational development project for 50 employees. Lead a talented team of analysts to uncover quick wins and long-term ROI on employee engagement and performance management for a tech company disrupting their industry.

Led a consumer analysis project to uncover brand perception and hidden consumer desires. Managed scope creep beyond the original statement of work while balancing the needs of the client.

Resume A	23%
Resume B	77%

(Source: Randomized choice options of the general population survey. N = 71)

Respondents reported picking resume B relative to resume A because of the clearly targeted objective, resume structure, targeted bullet points, contextual examples, and social proof.

Results are consistent across all other A/B split test.

> *"Over 75% of candidates are taken out of consideration*
> *before a human ever sees their resume."*
> – Amanda Augustine [38]

---

[38] http://money.com/money/5053350/resume-tips-free-template/

Consider the following example from an organizational change management resume:

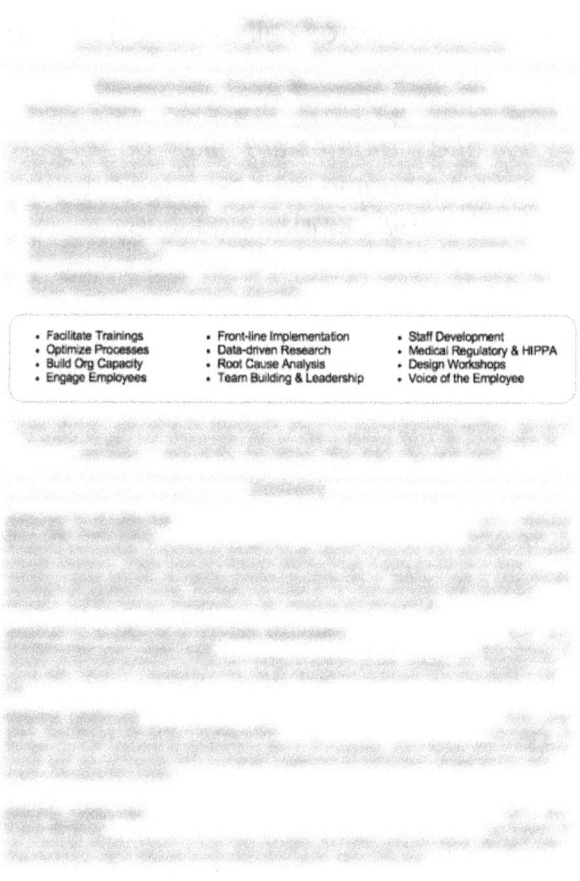

• Facilitate Trainings	• Front-line Implementation	• Staff Development
• Optimize Processes	• Data-driven Research	• Medical Regulatory & HIPPA
• Build Org Capacity	• Root Cause Analysis	• Design Workshops
• Engage Employees	• Team Building & Leadership	• Voice of the Employee

The highlighted 12 bullet points are more than just keywords from the job posting; they are targeted toward the role, and they speak to the industry. These 12 bullet points help us get past the ATS and are strategically placed above the fold of a screen so they'll also be read by hiring managers, too.

Chapter 11 Manufacture Credibility with Social Proof

In his widely popular book *Influence*, Robert Cialdini shares with the world his idea of Social Proof Theory, which is one of the most effective means of influencing consumers to buy something. The same tactic that Cialdini describes can be used on your resume to further boost your credibility with testimonials. To do this, use LinkedIn recommendations or quotes from your previous managers and colleagues to speak about you in the following format:

"[Your Name] was an outstanding service provider - timely, creative, proactive, and high quality output. I would recommend her/him without reservation."
– Name, Title, Company

What others say about you, your talent, your experience, and your know-how is infinitely more credible than anything you can say on your own behalf. This strategy will never go away. In fact, **submitting a resume without an endorsement** remains one of the biggest mistakes that job applicants make, let alone recent grads. It is one of the mistakes that gets repeated most often. Testimonials of people with different positions and authentic voices can be extremely powerful.

If you have several testimonials from previous professors, classmates, or managers, pick the one that came directly from a past manager or someone in a senior-level role, if possible. If you don't yet have one at that level, select one from the other recommendations that demonstrates your expertise for the job that you're interested in. If you don't have any testimonials at hand, here's what you need to do: Go get them!

If you are working on your resume right now, I want you to stop, fire up LinkedIn, and ask some of your previous managers and colleagues for their recommendations. If they don't have LinkedIn, send them an email asking for a letter of recommendation. I can't say it enough: **Social proof is crucial for your resume!**

Picture someone walking into a party and yelling: *"Hey everyone! You can relax now that I'm here. Come and see how fantastic I am!"* Our experiences tell us that people who do that aren't admired. The same can be said for personal branding. It's much more effective to have others speak enthusiastically on your behalf instead. You want to motivate others to cheerlead for you.

Hiring managers and HR reps will follow the behavior of others to avoid risk and maximize the certainty of obtaining value from their investment in you. Hiring managers and HR reps will always value the safe choice to protect their jobs, their company, and the paycheck that provides for their families. It really isn't surprising or unique that many people stick with the path of least resistance or the safe option.

How many of us, for example, change the default settings on our phones and computers? The answer is: not too many. Why? Because we don't need to. The original settings work just fine as they are. It's an easy and safe choice, and this allows our minds to continue operating on autopilot. In other words, we don't have to put forth too much mental or physical effort. Using that analogy, how can we reduce the amount of mental effort required of HR reps and hiring managers? How can we help them arrive at the decision to pick us? Yes, you got it — social proof!

Chapter 12 Sculpting Your Experience

Listing Past Roles

If you increased sales by a certain amount, put it down. If you had a positive impact on your team's life or if you improved a way that something was done in your last role, put it down. Don't hesitate. This is confident writing that needs to sell you. It's not gloating or bragging—it's communicating that you did X and, as a result, Y happened. It isn't enough to say you did something: You need to demonstrate how well you did it. Wherever you made an impact that was bigger, better, stronger, or faster for processes, team morale, revenue— anything that you helped improve—you need to write that down in lines five through nine.

Quantifying Examples

Here are some brief bullet point examples of writing that's confident and that will impress a hiring manager and allow you to build a narrative:

Decreased quarterly expenses from X% to $X

Slashed time in Accounts Receivable from 75 days to 41 days

Delivered project ahead of deadline by 5 days and under budget by $X

Be mindful of your word choice. Let's assume for a second that your starting annual salary is $70,000. If your resume is between 350 to 450 words, then you may think differently about each word being worth between $150.00 to $200.00. The Muse has put together a fairly robust set of power verbs that are proven to be among the best words to use when describing yourself: [39]

If you were in charge of a project or initiative from start to finish, skip "led" and instead try: Chaired | Controlled | Coordinated | Executed | Headed | Operated | Orchestrated | Organized | Oversaw | Planned | Produced | Programmed

And if you actually developed, created, or introduced that project into your company? Try: Administered | Built | Charted | Created | Designed | Developed Devised | Founded | Engineered | Established | Formalized | Formed | Formulated Implemented | Incorporated | Initiated | Instituted | Introduced | Launched Pioneered | Spearheaded

Hiring managers love candidates who've helped a team operate more efficiently or cost-effectively. To show just how much you saved, try: Conserved | Consolidated | Decreased | Deducted | Diagnosed | Lessened | Reconciled Reduced | Yielded

Along similar lines, if you can show that your work boosted the company's numbers in some way, you're

[39] https://www.themuse.com/advice/185-powerful-verbs-that-will-make-your-resume-awesome

bound to impress. In these cases, consider: Accelerated | Achieved | Advanced | Amplified | Boosted | Capitalized | Delivered Enhanced | Expanded | Expedited | Furthered | Gained | Generated | Improved Lifted | Maximized | Outpaced | Stimulated | Sustained

So, you brought your department's invoicing system out of the Stone Age and into civilization? Talk about the amazing changes you made at your office with these words: Centralized | Clarified | Converted | Customized | Influenced Integrated | Merged | Modified | Overhauled | Redesigned | Refined | Refocused Rehabilitated | Remodeled | Reorganized | Replaced | Restructured | Revamped | Revitalized | Simplified | Standardized | Streamlined | Strengthened | Updated Upgraded | Transformed

Instead of reciting your management duties, like "Led a team..." or "Managed employees..." show what an inspirational leader you were with terms like: Aligned | Cultivated | Directed | Enabled | Facilitated | Fostered | Guided | Hired | Inspired | Mentored | Mobilized | Motivated | Recruited | Regulated | Shaped Supervised | Taught | Trained | Unified | United

Were you "responsible for" a great new partner, sponsor, or source of funding? Try: Acquired | Forged | Navigated | Negotiated | Partnered | Secured

Because manning the phones or answering questions really means you're advising customers and meeting their needs, use: Advised | Advocated | Arbitrated | Coached | Consulted | Educated | Fielded | Informed | Resolved

Did your job include research, analysis, or fact-finding? Mix up your verbiage with these words: Analyzed | Assembled | Assessed | Audited | Calculated | Discovered | Evaluated | Examined | Explored | Forecasted | Identified Interpreted | Investigated | Mapped | Measured | Qualified | Quantified | Surveyed | Tested | Tracked

Was writing, speaking, lobbying, or otherwise communicating part of your gig? You can explain just how compelling you were with words like: Authored Briefed | Campaigned | Co-authored | Composed | Conveyed | Convinced | Corresponded | Counseled | Critiqued | Defined | Documented | Edited | Illustrated | Lobbied | Persuaded | Promoted | Publicized | Reviewed

Whether you enforced protocol or managed your department's requests, describe what you really did, better, with these words: Authorized | Blocked | Delegated | Dispatched | Enforced | Ensured | Inspected | Itemized | Monitored | Screened | Scrutinized | Verified

Did you hit your goals? Win a coveted department award? Don't forget to include that on your resume, with words like: Attained | Awarded | Completed | Demonstrated | Earned | Exceeded | Outperformed | Reached | Showcased | Succeeded | Surpassed | Targeted

(Power verb source: https://www.themuse.com/advice/185-powerful-verbs-that-will-make-your-resume-awesome)

When sports broadcasters review the resumes of baseball players who are being considered for the All-Star Game, they don't say: *"Oh, he was responsible for swinging the bat really hard, being a team player, and catching the baseball anytime it was near him."* No, they specifically quantify the player's performance in terms of results: home runs, base hits, RBIs, batting average, errors, etc. This example is just another way to remind you of an important point: **Shift from listing responsibilities to listing your results.**

Laszlo Bock, former SPV of People Operations at Google,[40] does a great job of quantifying with context for the role. He illustrates the evolution of rewriting what was originally listed in the following four examples:

Student Leader

What the student will usually put down on their resume: *Managed club budget*

Taking a second revision with context: *Managed $31,000 Spring 2014 budget and invested idle funds in appropriate high-yielding capital notes*

The student's final revision with further supporting context: *Managed $31,000 Spring 2014 budget and invested $10,000 in idle funds in appropriate high-yielding capital notes returning 5% over the year*

College Leadership Program

What the student will usually put down on their resume: *Member of Management Leadership for Tomorrow (MLT)*

---

[40] https://www.linkedin.com/pulse/20140929001534-24454816-my-personal-formula-for-a-better-resume/

The student's second revision with context: *Selected as one of 230 for 18-month professional development program for high-achieving diverse talent*

The student's final revision with further supporting context: *Selected as one of 230 participants nationwide for 18-month professional development program for high-achieving diverse talent based on leadership potential, ability to contribute to this MLT cohort, and academic success*

Professional Services Role

What the young professional will usually put down on their resume: *Responsible for negotiating service contracts with XYZ*

The young professional's second revision with context: *Negotiated 30% ($500k) reduction in costs with XYZ to perform post-delivery support*

The young professional's final revision with further supporting context: *Negotiated 30% ($500k) reduction in costs with XYZ to perform post-delivery support by designing and using results from an online auction of multiple vendors*

Account Representative or Sales Support

What an account rep will usually put down on their resume: *Achieved annual business plan commitments for volumes, model mix, wholesale revenue, selling expenses and brand*

The account rep's second revision with context and supporting evidence: *As a team member, contributed to*

21% increase in advertiser spend by achieving 158% of target number of customer contacts (80 contacts per week) and 192% of target interaction depth (20 minutes per customer)

What if you were a co-contributor in some big achievement? Simply state that. It's unrealistic to think that you achieved every accomplishment by yourself. Credit your team and yourself. Pay attribution to helping others as well as others helping you. This demonstrates that you're a team player and not a solo actor looking to feed your ego. This is often tough for many to balance with their resumes because 1) you want to market yourself, but 2) you don't feel like you're bragging. Kudos to your parents for raising you well! I find that a healthy approach is to blend projects in which you clearly led and accomplished the task on your own with other times when you contributed with other team members to achieve the goal.

Some companies want leaders, not sociopaths. At the same time, others want a blend of leadership and team playing. This will vary heavily based upon where in the organization you're applying.

Oh, and what about volunteer work? Should I list all of it?

In short, my answer is that it's a solid strategy and I recommend it. In a LinkedIn survey, 42% of hiring managers said that they consider volunteer work equivalent to full-time work experience, and 20% said they'd hired someone because of their volunteer experience.[41] Twenty-seven percent of job seekers are more likely to be hired, when unemployed, if they volunteer.

---

[41] https://blog.linkedin.com/2014/01/15/the-linkedin-volunteer-marketplace-connecting-professionals-to-nonprofit-volunteer-opportunities

So, volunteering is also a good way to hedge against gaps in employment.

Coursework, Conferences & Books

If you don't happen to have much experience, demonstrating your effort to gain experience can help and make up the difference. Listing additional coursework, classes enrolled in and passed, certificates, conferences you've attended, and books you've read on the topic are good items to include. Listing books you've read only works if you can show that you've read something like the top 10 or 20 books on Amazon about the topic. And, if you are going to present a reading list, those books need to be specialized and relevant to the role you're going after. Listing books from your book club will not be much help.

Empty Spaces

In design, empty areas are generally referred to as "white space," whether or not it's actually white. That space can help direct the reader's eye from a contrasting quiet area to an area of focus. Make good use of white space on your resume. The above two examples capture the extremes of resume design.

The resumes on the next page are blurred out because I want you to focus only on the areas of white space rather than on the content. It's pretty clear without seeing the content which resume is easier to read. If your resume is easier to read, then the HR rep and hiring manager are more inclined to read it. But even then, there is white space that is being neglected without symmetry to further capitalize on easier readability.

White space is a design concept that is necessary for

Resume with too much white space	Resume without white space
	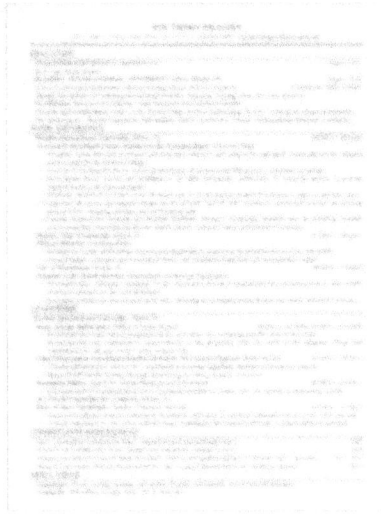

readability. Too much white space and you will lose precious real estate on your 8.5 x 11 resume. Too little and readability drops, rendering your resume useless. Copywriters and designers advocate for white space around headlines for the greatest impact. Your "headlines" are one of the key secrets of your resume: top third, targeted bullet points, key phrases, social proof, your experience, and your education.

Embrace the empty space

Bruce McCandless did the first ever spacewalk without being attached to the spacecraft in 1984.
He used a jet-propelled backpack to move around instead.
(Source: NASA. Photo ID: S84-27031 https://commons.wikimedia.org/wiki/File:Astronaut-in-space.jpg)

Breathing room in between

Since we are looking to maximize readability, design space between lines is critical. Too much or too little space decreases readability.

66 Tell me and I forget, teach me and I may remember, involve me and I learn 99 — Benjamin Franklin	66 Tell me and I forget, teach me and I may remember, involve me and I learn 99 — Benjamin Franklin
66 Tell me and I forget, teach me and I may remember, involve me and I learn 99 — Benjamin Franklin	In the box in the upper left quadrant there is little room for the quote to breathe with spacing that's too tight. The quadrant to the upper right gives just the right amount of breathing or "leading" as designers call it to maximize readability. The quadrant to the bottom left uses too much breathing room that can make it uncomfortable to read.

101

One Page Resume or Two?

The conventional wisdom is that if you have less than 10 years of experience you should use one page for your resume. And if you have a graduate degree or 10+ years of experience, then two pages will be a better fit... even though recent research actually suggests otherwise. Consider the following:

Hiring Rate: Two-Page resumes vs. One-Page resumes

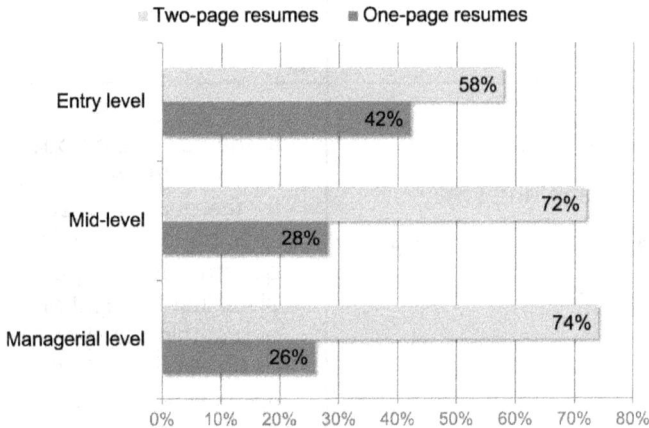

(Image source: https://www.resumego.net/research/one-or-two-page-resumes)

Although some recent data suggests that a two-page resume is ideal, this data assumes that the candidate has enough content with work experience, volunteer experience, education, etc. for two pages. Don't feel pressured to fill two pages if you don't have enough content yet. If your content does exceed one page, just make sure that you maintain your reader's interest. Again, this is a marketing campaign so if you can get away with one page then do so.

Highlight Multilingualism

If you speak a language other than English, make sure to include it on your resume, especially if you can read and write in other languages. You will want to specify what language you read, write, and speak, including your level of fluency and how relevant the language is for the role.

Examples:

Language	Language
Spanish (speak—conversational)	Spanish (read, write, and speak—native) (Link the percentage of customers doing business in a region and how you can help facilitate growth.)

Chapter 13 How You Present Your Education

Some resume writers will advocate putting your experience before your education, even if you have a strongly branded degree. In fact, in a YouTube video from Google on *"How to Work at Google – Resume Tips,"* they ask applicants to put education before work experience.[42] This makes sense given that the majority of entry-level tech hires are fresh from school, but that's not always the case. This could simply be Google's style. It might be valid for them, but if you have good, relevant job experience, by all means start your resume with job experience first and push your education to the bottom of your resume. Yet, if you are just starting out and have little experience do you want to lead with your education.

Your education section will include certificates, relevant courses outside of your degree, and any professional development. I've even seen awards and accomplishments listed that also work quite well.

Being precise about your education and your language use is the single best strategy to get past the ATS. For example, Taleo's ATS fails to grab common acronyms such as MBA or PMP, so you'll want to list Master of Business Administration (MBA) or Project Management Professional (PMP) to make sure your experience gets captured.

Q: What about my GPA?

---

[42] How to: Work at Google — Resume Tips https://www.youtube.com/watch?v=zrXZBkYzuZo

According to Josh Bernsin, while GPA and pedigree certainly play a role, they are far less important than you might think. Bernsin's research highlights the following:

> ...*a senior recruiter (he spent more than 20 years recruiting engineers) told me that after years of experience hiring people, the single biggest factor which predicts performance is "the experience of the recruiter." [Wait what?] What he found was that GPA, school, etc. had almost no correlation to success—but the very senior and very savvy recruiters had a sixth sense for "What it takes to be an A-Player."*[43]

So having a high GPA is commendable, but if you can demonstrate experience in the same area on your resume, sacrifice your GPA in favor of content that's relevant to the role for which you're applying.

It is worth noting, given the latest trend to round up education in Silicon Valley for those who started a degree but failed to complete it, that you should make sure that is clearly stated. Many people drop out to pursue other endeavors, which is completely okay. Yet, just be sure to clearly state a partially complete degree. Employers are starting to check by using the National Student Clearinghouse.[44]

What about that internship?

"It doesn't matter if the internship you performed was paid, unpaid, or for college credits. Experience is experience, and the skills you learned and the exposure you gained to your employer's industry during your college internship are worth

---

[43] Bernsin, Josh https://joshbersin.com/2012/05/making-the-job-search-work-the-science-of-fit/

[44] http://www.studentclearinghouse.org/

touting on your resume… the internship has taken the place of the entry-level job"[45] Here is an example below highlighting notable internship experience:

RELEVANT FINANCE EXPERIENCE

123 MANAGEMENT CONSULTING FIRM • Houston, TX (May-Aug. 2015)
Leading global business consulting and internal audit firm specializing in risk, advisory, and transaction services.

Process Intern: Responsible for defining internal business process issues, compiling information, and analyzing data in order to present solutions to team's clients. Built technical skills in general risk areas and helped clients review, document, evaluate, and test controls.
- **Ensured client achieved full compliance** with the Sarbanes-Oxley Act by performing a series of required tests.
- Helped **optimize client's payroll process** by researching and documenting departmental processes for management's review.

ABC DEFENSE & SPACE, CO. • Dallas, TX (Jun.-Aug. 2014)
Technology and innovation leader specializing in defense, security and civil markets throughout the world.

Finance Intern: Collaborated with a team of 10 to manage $135M financial portfolio for national defense programs. Responsible for analyzing cost models for element of cost reasonableness and provided models to function areas for feedback. Learned various transactions in SAP/BW to pull contract numbers and necessary data.
- **Achieved 96% forecast accuracy** by building and maintaining 14 cost curve models by product line that took into account the differences amongst production, spares, logistics, and repair contracts.
- Participated in a **Six Sigma project** to create a consistent process for issuing Individual Work Authorizations (IWAs).

(Image source: https://www.topresume.com/career-advice/does-internship-experience-count-as-professional-experience)

[45] https://www.topresume.com/career-advice/does-internship-experience-count-as-professional-experience

Here's a good example of a resume with limited experience:

ENTRY-LEVEL SALES & MARKETING ASSOCIATE

Recent graduate of a highly ranked university, with experience promoting brands and marketing products to businesses and consumers. Seeking opportunities to leverage project management, sales and integrated marketing skill set in a business development or account management capacity.

EDUCATION & TECHNICAL SKILLS

JAMES MADISON UNIVERSITY • Harrisonburg, VA (Jun 2014)
Bachelor of Arts in Organizational Communication • Major GPA: 3.45/4.00

Social Media (Facebook • Instagram • Twitter • Vine) • Factiva • Critical Mention
Vocus Marketing & PR Software • Windows and Apple Operating Systems

RELEVANT SALES & MARKETING EXPERIENCE

TOONEY COMMUNICATIONS • Philadelphia, PA (May 2013-Aug 2013)
Interactive marketing and advertising agency specializing in television, digital, out of home, and radio advertising.

Marketing and Public Relations Intern (May 2013-Aug 2013)
- Assembled press kits for eight clients, including Wendy's Restaurants, American Red Cross®, and Ford.
- Developed media lists for five account managers, utilizing tools such as Factiva, Critical Mention and Vocus.
- Created and pitched an integrated marketing campaign to five executives at Station XYZ news, which included account management, creative, media, and public relations tactics.
- Handled over 75 client calls with the account management team, ranging from project check-ins to inbound client inquiries, in a professional and personable manner.

PI SIGMA EPSILON • Harrisonburg, VA (Sep 2011-Present)
Only national, professional fraternal organization in sales, marketing, and management in the United States.

Member & Project Lead (Sep 2011-Present)
- Led a 14-person team to prepare and implement a marketing plan to sell PSE-branded t-shirts and hooded sweatshirts to JMU student body at $19 and $35 price points, respectively.
- Designed flyers and developed social media campaigns on Facebook and Instagram to promote products to target audience.
- Generated $1,300 sales for the organization within a two-month timeframe by marketing and personally selling over 50 pieces of apparel throughout campus.

LEADERSHIP ACTIVITIES

JMU KIJIJI LEADERSHIP PROGRAM • Harrisonburg, VA (Sep 2011-May 2014)
Program geared towards enhancing JMU students' leadership skills and developing "Citizens of Influence" through group exercises, activities and volunteer opportunities. Students must apply and be accepted into the program.

Participant (Sept 2011-May 2014)
- Created an after-school mentoring program with two other program participants to help middle school children cope with bullying and self-image issues.
- Successfully enrolled 25 pairs of JMU students and middle school students in the program's pilot.

JAMES MADISON UNIVERSITY RECREATION CENTER (UREC) • Harrisonburg, VA (Jan 2011-Present)
Center dedicated to the promotion and advancement of healthy lifestyles through education and participation.

Official, UREC Intramural Sports Program (Jan 2011-Present)
- Developed crisis management techniques to ease dissatisfied competitors.
- Promoted and represented sportsmanship and teamwork in all facets of sporting events.

(Image source: https://www.topresume.com/career-advice/make-a-great-resume-with-no-work-experience)

Chapter 14 Bringing it all Together with Machine Learning

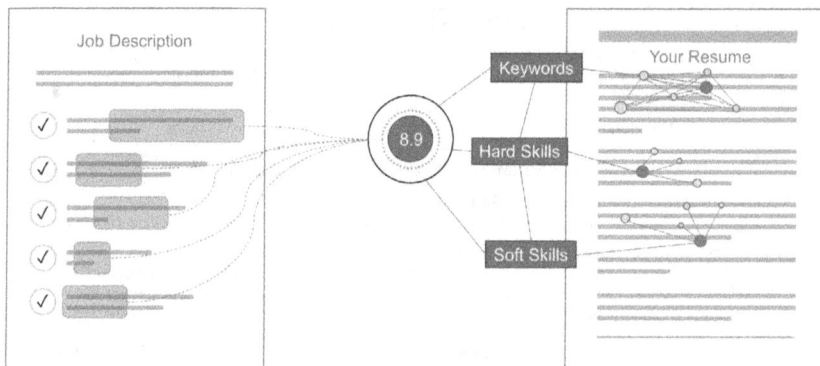

At this point are you ready to bring it all together. After looking through several job descriptions you should have a good idea of what hard skills, soft skills, and keywords are showing up the most across your industry but also for the job you're interested in. Now you'll want to dramatically improve your chances of landing an interview by running your resume through either https://resumeworded.com/ or www.jobscan.co

At the time of writing, Jobscan is offering five free scans before requiring a subscription; ResumeWorded is unlimited.

Paste your resume.

Paste the entire job description text. Exclude the 'About company' section but include the job title.

Clear resume

Clear job description

SCAN

(Image source www.jobscan.com)

Here's how we calculated your score

We've run over twenty checks on your resume. They can be grouped
into these four categories - here's how you did in each.

IMPACT ❓	BREVITY ❓	STYLE ❓	SOFT SKILLS ❓
40	46	58	100
NEEDS WORK	NEEDS WORK	NEEDS WORK	EXCELLENT

(Image source https://resumeworded.com)

MATCH RATE

Guide Me

Add more missing skills (indicated by ✗) into your resume to increase your match rate to 80% or above. ❓

38%

ATS FINDINGS
✔ 4 / 7   ✗ 3 / 7

RECRUITER FINDINGS
✔ 2 / 4   ⚠ 2 / 4

SKILLS MATCH
✔ 12 / 46   ✗ 34 / 46

FORMAT CHECKS ❓
✔ 1 / 2   ⚠ 1 / 2

COVER LETTER CHECKS ❓
✔ 0 / 0   ✗ 0 / 0

(Image source www.jobscan.com)

The real strength of machine learning tools is not just being able to accurately see where your resume is deficient but to suggest the right keywords. Jobscan does go a step further to analyze millions of job descriptions to provide suggested phrases and keywords to include on your resumes, assuming you possess the skill set.

SKILL	VARIATIONS ❓	RESUME	JOB DESCRIPTION
		12	6
	○	10	5
	○	5	4
	○	6	4
	○	2	2
		2	2
		1	- Predicted Skill ❓
		1	- Predicted Skill ❓

(Image source www.jobscan.com)

Each organization has its own culture, word choice, and ATS. Ignoring that fact can be detrimental to your chances of advancing to the interview stage.

Bear with me a moment even if this seems rather obvious. If you happen to think of yourself as creative, that's excellent. But let's say that the organization you're interested in uses the word "entrepreneurial" to describe the role instead of the word "creative"— then it's best to relabel how you describe your creative talents. This is one of the things that impresses me with both ResumeWorded and Jobscan for just this reason. They essentially help you translate your perception of yourself into their tribal language based upon the job description and the millions of job descriptions they have of an industry:

> *...many employers are trying to stand out by being cutesy... and using vague language... when you say "coding ninja," you're not going to match against "java developer." If you say "spreadsheet guru," you're going to miss the people with "Excel expertise."* [46]

There are dozens of ATS programs yet one example is the ATS Jobvite which doesn't consistently parse PDF files upon submission so you'll want to use a .doc, docx (Word Document) or a plain text file instead of a PDF when applying through Jobvite. For an applicant who is used to applying only with PDF versions of their resume, this is very practical advice.

---

[46] https://www.theatlantic.com/health/archive/2019/06/looking-for-a-job-americas-listings-are-inscrutable/591616/

Let Word Clouds Guide You

If you don't have the cash to dish out on ResumeWorded or Jobscan, no worries as word clouds can help. What kinds of words and phrases should you include in your resume? Try this strategy that uses a word cloud and existing job descriptions. For this example, we will use three different job descriptions for a project manager across separate industries to get a broad sense of how project management is being thought of in the current labor market.

(Image source: www.wordclouds.com)

There are two primary word cloud generators: Wordle and Wordclouds. For our example we'll be using Wordclouds. If you use Firefox or Internet Explorer, you may need to update your Java settings. Chrome and Safari usually don't have any problems. The output from Wordclouds will be a word cloud that will make the most- used words larger relative to the others. I suggest doing the following:

1) Pull three job titles for the role you're considering from <u>across different industries</u> and enter the job qualifications and descriptions into a Wordclouds box

2) Pull three job titles from <u>within an industry</u> and put the qualifications and descriptions into Wordclouds

3) Finally, put the qualifications and descriptions of the job you're targeting into Wordclouds to compare the outputs side by side

Given the three positions placed into Wordclouds and based upon the output from the word cloud, we can expect that some of the phrases in our resume need to have the following words: project, team, scrum, management, and managing.

It doesn't matter how beautiful your resume looks if it doesn't have relevant keywords and phrases that market YOU. If it doesn't, your resume is just going to sit in the ATS without progression.

Sort by: weight a-z

25	project
14	business
12	experience
12	work
11	SAP
10	projects
10	teams
9	team

Also, pay attention to the order in which criteria are presented in JDs (Job Descriptions). Usually, the top three bullet points under the required responsibilities and experience will be of heightened importance to the hiring manager.

Note the difference between the singular vs. plural count of the words "project" and "projects." The same can be seen with "team" and "teams." The word cloud algorithm is very precise, so be sure to account for similarities when perceiving word count.

What if you've already applied for the position?

I've personally tracked my own progress on applications and when I've received nothing but radio silence. I then restructured my resume, used Jobscan to make it past the ATS, and reapplied to the same role resulting in the HR recruiter reaching out for an interview and thanking me for reapplying, being persistent, and taking the time to provide more context to my resume. So if you've been rejected or haven't heard back, don't count yourself out! This is why it is important to not only tailor your resume but to also keep track of where you applied, what resume did you use, and the results (or absence of any).

The radio silence and rejections are nothing more than feedback loops. For example, SpaceX engineers don't take course corrections personally when they send out commands to have a rocket alter its path for a successful landing, and neither should you. The sting of rejection hurts, no doubt. And you may even feel like not wanting to change course at all, but life happens and things that are out of our control will alter the direction. So, take rejection as a data point and do your best to stay positive. Like a rocket, you're moving forward regardless, and you may just need small adjustments to get on track.

Brian Acton did just that. Five years after being denied for previous jobs, Acton sold his startup WhatsApp to Facebook for $16 billion.[47]

Brian Acton @brianacton · 3 Aug 2009
Facebook turned me down. It was a great opportunity to connect with some fantastic people. Looking forward to life's next adventure.

434   10K   8.3K

Brian Acton @brianacton · 23 May 2009
Got denied by Twitter HQ. That's ok. Would have been a long commute.

80   2.3K   2.0K

(Image source: https://twitter.com/brianacton?lang=en)

Hidden Keywords

Resume hacks once went around the Internet that tried to create an advantage for applicants by stuffing their resumes with keywords hidden in white text. The white text would make them invisible to the human eye (because of the white background) but visible to an electronic resume scanner or ATS. The intent of this ploy was to not only reach the top of

---

[47] https://www.wsj.com/articles/facebook-to-buy-whatsapp-for-16-billion-1392847766

the resume pile, but also to create the impression that the candidate needed to be interviewed. The sly approach may have worked early on for some, but HR reps and applicant tracking software are now hip to this and will immediately disqualify a candidate for taking this approach. My advice is: Don't do it.

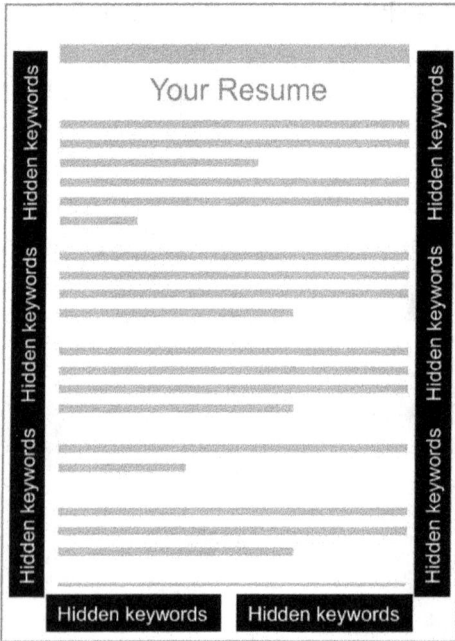

Hidden keywords

Your Resume

Hidden keywords

Hidden keywords

Hidden keywords

Hidden keywords

Hidden keywords

Hidden keywords

Hidden keywords

Hidden keywords

For illustrative purposes I've filled in the text boxes of hidden keywords in white font so you can get an idea of how people stuff keywords around their resume to game the ATS.

Again, very creative, but I don't recommend it.

Chapter 15 Tell Me Lies, Tell Me Sweet Little Lies

© MARK ANDERSON, WWW.ANDERTOONS.COM

ANDERSON UPHOLSTERY

"Excellent padding on your resume!"

(Image source: Mark Anderson – www.andertoons.com)

A recent survey by GoBankingRates suggested younger audiences are twice as likely as other generations to embellish parts of their resumes. The top three: work experience, dates of employment, and job title. The justification from the embellishment is to hide gaps in work experience.

Survey Question: If you have lied on your resume, what factors did you lie about? Select all that apply.[48]

Answer Choices	Percentage of Respondents
Your work experience	38%
Dates of employment	31%
Your job title at your previous role	16%
Your reference(s)	15%
Your college education	11%
Your responsibilities at your previous role	7%
Your GPA	4%
Your internship experience	2%

Note: Responses are from Americans who have admitted to lying on their resumes.

(Image source: https://www.gobankingrates.com/making-money/jobs/why-americans-lie-on-resumes/#6)

> "It's often during recruitment, even before a person has stepped foot inside an organization, that the lying starts. As candidates, we conform to who we think we ought to be in the eyes of an employer—in everything from our [resume], the way we dress, our attitudes and the questions we feel appropriate to ask or not ask to the stories we choose to tell about ourselves. ... [T]he recruitment process is often an uncomfortable dance of two partners wearing high heels to look taller, tight clothes to tuck the belly in, and so much makeup that you would not recognize them on a normal day."[49]

Using tools like Jobscan and ResumeWorded can certainly help you compete, but it also makes lying a lot easier even though it won't replace skills and experience. I can already see these resume tools becoming so mainstream in a few years'

---

[48] https://www.gobankingrates.com/making-money/jobs/why-americans-lie-on-resumes/#5

[49] Laloux, Frederic. Reinventing Organizations: A Guide to Creating Organizations Inspired by the Next Stage of Human Consciousness

time that hiring managers will evolve to no longer trust resumes.

Before that happens, job applicants can expect a bit more scrutiny to validate skills. Hiring managers will press candidates for evidence of skills beyond claims of skill on a resume or LinkedIn profile. So, don't be surprised if a hiring manager asks for proof of skill. For example, if the job description requires phone sales or conversational phone skills, you might be asked to leave a voicemail. We can see more of this through screening tools like Pymetrics in a game form to match candidates with teams.

> *"Resume padding happens at all levels of employment, as indicated by the HireRight survey. While more often associated with front-line employees, former Yahoo CEO Scott Thompson was forced to resign his position on May 13, 2012, after shareholders and company leaders became aware that his degree was inaccurate on his resume. In her May 2012 CNN article "Resume padding: inconsequential or inexcusable?" Emanuella Grinberg noted that false reports of advanced degrees such as MBAs are common."[50]*

Diploma mills and credential fabrication is a one-billion-dollar industry. As of the publication of this book, federal prosecutors are going after two Hollywood actresses and a CEO for similar behavior.[51] "More than half of all new PhDs in the US are fake … and even more disturbing, an extrapolation of the percentage of people holding fake diplomas in the medical field revealed potentially 2 million 'bogus practitioners.'"[52]

---

[50] https://work.chron.com/resume-padding-6500.html

[51] https://www.forbes.com/sites/zackfriedman/2019/03/12/hollywood-celebrities-charged-in-major-college-admissions-scandal/#51e928761dc5

[52] https://www.cbsnews.com/news/your-md-may-have-a-phony-degree/

For those who have ceremonially graduated but have a couple of classes yet to finish before actual degree completion, be up front about it. Language such as "expected completion by [date]" can help. Details matter, especially where your integrity is concerned. You may have a good reason for not finishing your degree (taking care of family, finances, work) -- hiring managers understand that -- be honest and authentic.

> *"...demonstrate that you're still dedicated to earning those credentials, such as enrolling in a program to finish your degree, or getting certified in your field. Saying, 'I know I don't have the credential right now, but I'm just X-credits away from a master's, and I would be glad to promise you that I will go back to school and finish the degree,' builds credibility. Or sometimes you can sit for a certification in your industry, where you don't necessarily need to have the full degree. Then you can say, 'I don't have my masters in HR, but I do have my SHRM (Society for Human Resource Management) certification."[53]*

In the same vein we can see tools like Crosschq being developed to catch inconsistencies with candidates and to protect company culture:

> *The program has candidates rate themselves on various factors like attention to detail and self motivation, and also has their references rate the candidate on the same things. The rating system is on a five-point, "OK to great" scale. The technology then compares the ratings, and triangulates the results with the job skills the*

---

[53] https://www.marketwatch.com/story/dont-make-the-same-critical-resume-mistake-as-disgraced-florida-politician-melissa-howard-2018-08-19

employer values.[54]

Make sure that your references can speak directly to your skill set, experience, and job titles. Having friends and former colleagues boast beyond expectations can hurt you at this phase, so make sure you get your facts straight with each one of your referring contacts.

Job Titles & Tact

If you're applying to individual contributor roles below the executive level and you have CEO, Founder, or Entrepreneur titles in your resume, be prepared to face a few hurdles:

1. Should you choose to keep those titles on your resume, be prepared to defend the accuracy of the titles or face faster rejection. Here's why: Despite the validity of your title and experience, if you're applying for roles below the executive level, you will be perceived as coming after the department head's job or any of the executives' — especially in a startup. That's not a risk that a hiring manager is willing to take.

2. CEO, Founder, or Entrepreneur titles can give the perception that you might be full of yourself and perceived as a flight risk if you don't move up fast enough in promotion.

3. If CEO, Founder, or Entrepreneur titles currently reflect what you're spending your time on, it may suggest that you won't be fully committed to the role you're applying for and may even pull resources to focus on your own business ventures.

---

[54] https://www.marketwatch.com/story/how-ai-is-catching-people-who-cheat-on-their-diets-job-searches-and-school-work-2019-06-10

That is why using any of those titles on your resume may make you want to rethink a title rebrand. As Brenda Bernstein author of *How to Write a Killer LinkedIn Profile* says, *"If you've done the job, you can claim the job title."* And regardless of what title you choose to rebrand with, make sure that it's consistent across your resume and LinkedIn profile.

Here is a real-life example of a red flag for a hiring manager:

Resume		LinkedIn
2018 - 03 – present	**Chief Operating Officer (Volunteer)**	**Volunteer Coordinator** Jan 2019 – Present · 7 mos

The difference between the titles at the same company (blurred out) and incongruent dates at the company between the resume and LinkedIn profile creates confusion and fast-tracks the resume for rejection.

If you're going to give yourself a title, make sure that it reflects the nature of your volunteer, freelance, contract, or consulting work. Self-employment is great, just make sure that it represents you well.

Chapter 16 You Need An Inside Advocate

How People Landed Jobs

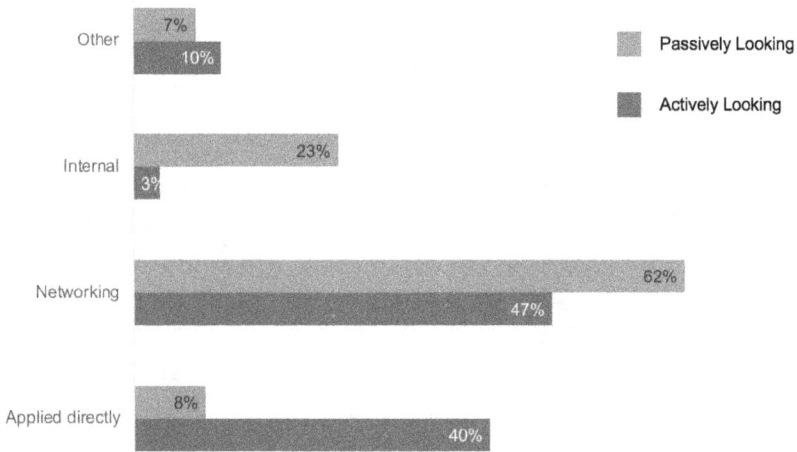

Other — 7% (Passively Looking), 10% (Actively Looking)

Internal — 23% (Passively Looking), 3% (Actively Looking)

Networking — 62% (Passively Looking), 47% (Actively Looking)

Applied directly — 8% (Passively Looking), 40% (Actively Looking)

Legend: Passively Looking, Actively Looking

(Source: https://www.linkedin.com/pulse/new-survey-reveals-85-all-jobs-filled-via-networking-lou-adler)

Now that you have your resume updated and polished, it's time to line up the delivery. Before blasting your resume off to the jobs you've tailored it for (I don't recommend blasting your resume out), you first want to line up an inside advocate. You may wonder why some people are able to secure top positions in an organization so easily, especially when they are not particularly skilled. It is likely that they've built up relationships and created inside advocates. Your network is your net worth.

At least 70% of jobs are not even listed

What is an inside advocate? A person within the company or organization who can refer you for the role or directly to the hiring manager. A referral is the best way to get a job in the current market, hands down. Matt Youngquist, career coach and president of Career Horizons, says, *"at least 70 percent, if not 80 percent, of jobs are not published… yet most people spend a majority of their time surfing the web for their next opportunity when they should be out networking."*[55] When you're referred, your chances increase tenfold over simply sending off your resume. This strategy, combined with your fresh new resume, greatly improves your odds of landing an interview. Not only that, being referred has been reported to net candidates with roles that they're much happier with.

Reach out to an employee on LinkedIn in the department you're looking to get into. Kindly introduce yourself and see if they would be open to a brief 15 minute call. Be very clear and mindful of their time. Once you get them on the phone this is where you'll need to be a conversationalist. Thank them for taking the time. Ask them about their job and why they like working there. See if they can speak to the culture. Use this at your own discretion, yet I'd recommend waiting a few days to a week before asking for a referral to the hiring manager.

If you're unable to connect with anyone in the company, then an email with the subject line "Informational interview" is a good strategy to help you secure a contact. But be careful in

---

[55] https://www.cnbc.com/2018/05/24/resume-is-only-10-percent-of-why-a-company-hires-you-focus-on-this-instead.html

your approach. If you come off in your cold introductory email to be self-serving, that can turn off a potential advocate.

This strategy depends upon if you've already applied or not. Ideally if you have yet to apply do you want to see if the hiring manager is up to grab a quick cup of coffee (on you of course). Yet, if you have already applied, then it is a good idea to find an inside advocate. And yes, feel free to invite to invite other employees in the company out for coffee, too. If you don't drink coffee then tea is a good substitute.

Chapter 17 Before You Click Apply

"Far too often it's a spray and pray approach..."
- Nancy Soni, PathMatch [56]

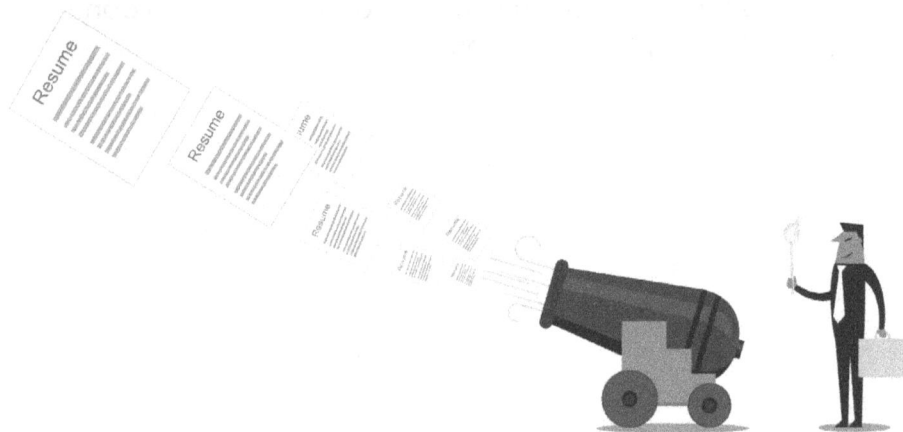

How you apply for jobs is just as important as the time that you spent crafting your resume. Don't blast your resume at every job that catches your eye: Instead, carefully target the company and role that interests you. The same is true for LinkedIn. LinkedIn's "Easy Apply" might as well be "Easy Rejection."[57] It is quite difficult to stand out from the crowd when you're using Easy Apply because guess what everyone else is doing? Yes, they're also applying with little effort and then moving on to their day.

---

[56] Interview with Nancy Soni on Sept 20, 2019

[57] https://medium.com/@thomashillhouse/what-hiring-managers-see-when-you-easy-apply-on-linkedin-61709431ecad

If you want to get noticed by the hiring manager, you must bypass Easy Apply and go directly to the company's career page and apply there. This not only increases your chances; it is favorable to hiring managers and recruiters, too. Their perception will be that you made the effort of visiting the website and applying directly rather than passively as many others have done.

The company's career page is two times more effective for hiring than job boards.[58] Recent research from Jobvite provides evidence from various sources of hiring and the hire percentage and effectiveness rate. In short, internal company resources are the most effective.

Source Name	Hire Count	Hire Percentage	Applications	Application Percentage	Effectiveness
Career Site	69,502	28.93%	4,993,677	34.93%	0.83
Job Boards	45,928	19.12%	7,060,680	49.38%	0.39
Entered by Recruiter	31,172	12.98%	280,870	1.96%	6.61
Referral	29,458	12.26%	376,594	2.63%	4.66
Internal Mobility *	19,242	8.01%	74,273	0.52%	15.42
Agency	9,425	3.92%	201,341	1.41%	2.79
Hiring Manager	6,425	2.67%	19,760	0.14%	19.35
Email Campaign	778	0.32%	20,212	0.02%	2.29
Custom Campaign	362	0.15%	2,569	0.02%	8.39
Federated Search	237	0.10%	3,233	0.01%	4.36
Resume Search	102	0.04%	1,924	0.01%	3.82
Notifications	97	0.04%	1,587	0.01%	3.64
Social Media Shares	57	0.02%	600	0.00%	5.65

*In previous reports, "Internal Mobility" was called "Internal Hire/Application."

(Image source: Jobvite 2019 Recruiting Benchmark Report)

---

[58] https://www.jobvite.com/wp-content/uploads/2019/03/2019-Recruiting-Benchmark-Report.pdf

Here is an example of how the ATS will organize candidates:

Candidate **A**	APPLIED ⌄	Careers Page	
Candidate **B**	APPLIED ⌄	LinkedIn	Job site
Candidate **C**	APPLIED ⌄	Glassdoor	Job site

(Image source: Lever)

Don't be tempted by the easiness of a one-click button. You want to be Candidate A, applying directly through the company's careers page.

What About Timing?

According to TopResume, "...some employers will only consider the first 50% (30 out of 62) of job applications that make it past their ATS. That means, even if you possess all the skills and experience you need for a job, you could lose out if you don't apply early enough."[59]

Beware of Browser Tracking

Google searches, Facebook likes, and any webpage that you visit are being followed. Most of the tracking on your internet behavior is being done by marketers. Third-party advertisements have tracking cookies that allow the algorithm to construct a decent profile of who you are based on your browsing habits and your interests. Employers have a financial incentive to know who they are hiring before making them an offer, and that is why some will deploy the same tactics by pulling cookies from your browser to see if your online behavior lines up with the type of person whom they want working for them. This is partly what spurred the European Union's GDPR (General Data Protection Regulation) to limit the kinds of user data that companies can collect and share.

Despite GDPR, some minimal tracking can still be done. So, in order to control your personal brand and how you're perceived, apply to jobs in a separate browser like Firefox or Chrome. Whatever your default browser is, I'd suggest using something else that is separate when you apply for jobs, and that's it.

---

[59] https://www.topresume.com/career-advice/the-early-bird-gets-the-job-the-best-time-to-submit-your-resume

Well, if that's the case, then a good question to consider is: Why not just use privacy mode in Firefox or incognito mode in Chrome?

Chrome	Firefox
	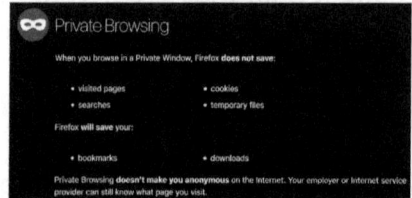

Unfortunately, using incognito and private browsing still allows some minimal tracking to take place. It's best to use a different browser altogether to apply for jobs and submit resumes, preferably a browser that you rarely use at all. And if you have used a separate browser in the past, make sure to delete all of your cookies prior to applying. If not, companies like Evolv will make an impression of you, according to a recent article in *The Economist:*.

> Evolv, a company that monitors recruitment and workplace data, has suggested that there are better ways to identify the right candidate for a job [based upon internet browsing behavior]. It analyzed 3m data points from over 30,000 employees, comparing traits of applicants with those of existing employees, to determine which traits are most indicative of reliability, trustworthiness and suitability for particular jobs. Among

other things, its analysis found that those applicants who have bothered to install new web browsers on their computers (such as Mozilla's Firefox or Google's Chrome) perform better and stay in their posts for 15% longer, on average, than those who use the default pre-installed browser that came with their machine (ie, Internet Explorer on a Windows PC and Safari on an Apple Mac).[60]

(Image source: Dilbert - Scott Adams, 9-5-2013. License through Andrews McMeel Syndication)

Keep Your Resume File Name Simple

Use the KISS methodology: Keep It Simple, Silly. Oftentimes people name their resume with the job title along with the company as the file name on their resume. If you do that, please stop. HR reps know what position you're applying for in a company. Instead, you will want to name your resume with one of the following options:

1) Firstname.lastname(date).docx or .PDF
2) Lastname.firstname.2020.docx or .PDF
3) First initial.lastname.docx or .PDF

[60] https://www.economist.com/the-economist-explains/2013/04/10/how-might-your-choice-of-browser-affect-your-job-prospects

Your Resume on Mobile

In case you want another reason for using the suggested resume style in this book, here it is. Have you ever considered what your resume looks like on mobile iOS or Android? If you haven't, no worries—it's not a thought that we often consider when thinking about resumes because it's assumed that resume viewing happens only on desktop.

Many hiring managers and recruiters, however, are on their phones checking email between meetings, on a flight home, or during a break at a conference. So, your resume must be mobile friendly. Saving your resume in the most recent version of Adobe PDF is your first and best strategy to control for mobile viewing. The second is using the previously suggested resume style so you have the most optimal white space.

How can you be sure what it will look like? Try this: Email your resume to yourself and then see what it looks like. This will give you a chance to be sure that there is no funky formatting or that you accidentally left off a blank second page.

Two-page
resume

Two-page
resume
with second
page missing

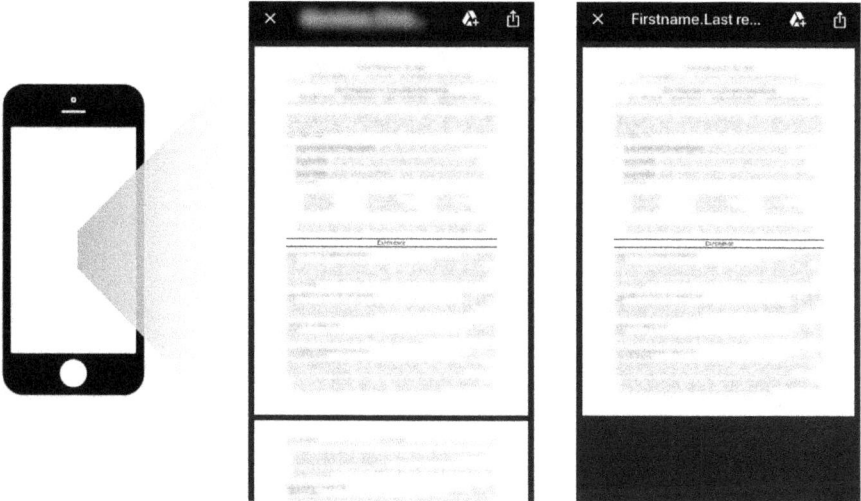

Don't Bother With References

There is no need to <u>state references upon request</u>. Both the HR rep and hiring manager are aware of this. If they want them, they'll certainly ask, and they don't need you to remind them on your resume. In short, we want to save space by not stating the obvious.

Part Two

Chapter 18 Changing the Rules

A covert way to get your resume seen

This secret tactic gives you a 98% chance of getting into the hiring manager's hands and getting opened.[61] Ready? Here it is:

Step 1) Grab a plain white #10 envelope, which is measured 4 ⅛ inches by 9 ½ inches

Step 2) Handwrite your mailing address (omit your name) and the hiring manager's name, title, and company address

Step 3) Fold your resume into three sections and insert into your #10 envelope

Step 4) Use a First-Class Stamp or Forever Stamp and drop it in the mail

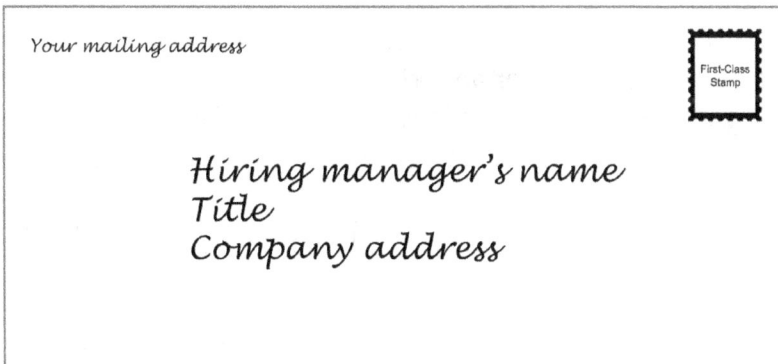

"Envelopes addressed by hand often outperform all others in controlled split tests."[62]

---

[61] The Ultimate Sales Letter, by Dan Kennedy
[62] The Ultimate Sales Letter, By Dan Kennedy

This strategy not only bypasses the ATS, it ensures that you will distinctively stand out from your competition. Directly mailing a hiring manager doesn't guarantee an interview, however, similar tests have shown that it does pull a higher response rate than any other digital medium.[63] Getting an interview depends on what you say in your resume, so just make sure that your resume is rock solid before mailing.

As a hiring manager, I was never swayed by a cover letter, and many of them always sounded the same to me. There is only a 17% chance your cover letter will be read.[64] Not the best odds. I'm not one to suggest them, but if you decide to use this mailing strategy you will want to include a brief and targeted cover letter with your resume. Because in this direct mail approach do your chances dramatically increase of your cover letter being read.

Moving Away From the Conventional Wisdom

"If everyone's playing the same game by the same set of rules then it's time to change the rules of the game" – Bernie Jaworski[65]

Consider the following story from Lindsey Kirchoff, a Tufts University student who changed the rules and got creative. The following excerpt courtesy of Mark W. Schaefer, author of *KNOWN* [66] (which I highly recommend):

> *It was a very scary time to think about being a college graduate.*
>
> *At the university, I minored in Entrepreneurial Leadership Studies and learned about inbound marketing. Instead of*

---

[63] ANA/DMA Response Rate Report 2018

[64] https://www.thejobnetwork.com/this-is-why-your-resume-was-rejected-infographic/

[65] Organic Growth Playbook AMA by Bernie Jaworski

[66] KNOWN: The handbook for building and unleashing your personal brand in the digital age by Mark W. Schaefer

interrupting customers with advertising messages, inbound marketing encourages the use of social media and content to get found and build relationships with customers. It seemed to me that this was a good way to look for a job, too. Instead of just sending out resumes and saying, "Hey, look at me!" I decided to apply those same principles and create something of value that people would actually want to see.

I needed to show what I could do, not just tell people, so I created a blog called, "How to Market to Me." I simply wrote about my observations on marketing and advertising campaigns that I thought hit the mark, or missed the mark, with millennials. Writing these articles gave me a new sense of purpose, and a title: millennial marketing blogger. Even though I wasn't employed, I was working and publishing on LinkedIn and my blog gave me the platform to show it.

I also made a concerted effort to build a specific audience of people who might hire me. Rather than applying to any job opening, I narrowed my focus to interesting companies I found through blogging and researching my industry. By publishing on LinkedIn I hoped these individuals would start to see some of my work.

And they did. Not only did Kirchoff find employment shortly after graduation, because of her blog, she became known and sought-after.

- *She was invited to keynote an automotive conference with a talk about millennial car-buying behaviors.*
- *She was quoted in The Los Angeles Times for insights into millennial habits.*

- Campbell's soup's CEO recruited her to participate in a millennial think tank.
- She collaborated with futurologist Faith Popcorn as a member of her Brain Reserve.
- She was featured in self-help author Paul Angone's book *101 Secrets for Your 20s*.

Lindsey's story is an example of bridging two skill sets to create a point of differentiation.

Here's another example from a clever candidate who applied for a role in a leadership coaching firm.

> *"I knew I had to work for them," he says. So, after a preliminary phone interview, during which he learned that the team was unhappy with their current digital marketing, he arrived at the in-person interview with a search engine optimization audit, showing everything they did wrong. He included a detailed list of SEO errors and opportunities to improve their online presence, as well as step-by-step instructions to make the necessary changes. "I told them that even if they didn't hire me to do the work, the report was theirs to use as they please. They were 'intrigued' by me and said they would be having a meeting to discuss an even larger role than the one I was interviewing for," he says.*[67]

After 90 days of implementing this book's strategies, if you haven't had any good results, it is fair to switch up your strategy. Most definitely.

---

[67] https://www.fastcompany.com/90428875/should-you-try-a-wacky-job-application-strategy

By that I mean bypassing HR, the application, and the traditional approach of applying for a job. Essentially you will be creating a new campaign. This means not waiting or hoping for a role to be posted at the company you want but going after what you want!

Create five to 10 slides, no more and no less, in PowerPoint and then convert those slides into a PDF to strategically personalize and distribute. What you create in those five or 10 slides is critical to the success of this covert campaign.

Why? Because you're essentially creating a pitch deck for targeted hiring managers. I'd suggest initially starting with three companies to target; and you'll want to be very clear and deliberate about these companies because you need to explain why you're a good fit in relation to their values, culture, and what you bring to the table. I don't suggest picking more than three because you'll need to go deep and do some homework about them. More than three is just too overwhelming.

Take a chance

Does this approach seem a bit audacious? Yes it can be, but it doesn't have to be. Again, if the previous approaches presented in this book are not working, you need to take a different approach to achieve your goal. Get creative. When you are creative it takes you to a whole other place. The truth is competition is the opposite of creativity. Competition can prevent you from thinking creatively to make all concepts of competition obsolete.[68] Admittedly this strategy can feel awkward at first because it's not something that's taught or commonly known. But this is the same way that startups get funded. Feel free to edit and adopt the following email script:

---

[68] Terry Crews on competition from Tribe of Mentors by Tim Ferriss

Hi [hiring managers name],

I came across [name of role] and I'm quite interested. To demonstrate my value I've put together the following [PDF slides or webpage link] to show my interest and capability in being considered for the team.

[Place in your brief bio and the relevancy you have for the role here.]

Thank you for your time, and I'd very much welcome next steps.

[Your name]

The following is a great example provided by a job-seeker named Nina. She took the same proactive approach but in a webpage form at: http://www.nina4airbnb.com Nina's analysis provides credibility and authority for her skill set and demonstrates that she understands Airbnb's market. All around impressive!

A webpage is certainly welcome, but it's much more time-consuming and takes a bit of risk to put all of your eggs in one basket when targeting a single company. You can go ahead and do this (at your own risk), but I'd argue that creating between five and 10 PDF slides instead will provide you with material that you can leverage and apply towards other firms.

Hey, I'm Nina!

San Francisco, California.
Member since March 2013. Host since July 2014.

I want to work at Airbnb. I realize thousands of other very talented people do as well, so to show the kind of value I'd bring to the team, I've decided to be proactive and have analyzed the global tourism market to give you my two cents on where Airbnb should focus next.

Please scroll through the report, and get in touch when you're done!

Scroll to Learn More

Learn More about Me

- Connect With Me on Twitter
  @ninasmyfish
- Find me on LinkedIn
  To see what else I've worked on
- Read My Blog
  Just for fun

(Image source: www.nina4airbnb.com)

Though Nina has a nice photo, I'd also advise that you don't include one with your slides or webpage if you create one. The casual vibe that Nina's photo conveys just might work for Airbnb, but it may not for other companies, so use caution. Again, Nina did her homework about her audience and avoided using a super corporate-style or formal image. Everything about her webpage is worth studying in detail if you plan to take this route in your job hunt.

Inspirational stories

While I was on my own journey helping students and picking up the experiences that have supplied the content for this book, I sometimes turned to other people's stories when my hopes were sagging and I needed support. If you need inspiration (aside from this book), check out the following sources:

How I Got My Job
(http://howigotjob.com/)
Step-by-step stories from recent grads about how they landed their jobs. This is a terrific website that continually updates with new stories so you're guaranteed to find something that you never read before.

How I Hustled to Get the Perfect Job
https://medium.com/@inaherlihy/how-i-hussled-to-get-the-perfect-job-bd24e74188ae
Ina Herlihy, an ambitious Scripps College graduate, documents her hustle in extensive detail. You'll read her threads with various contacts and learn about the various action steps she took at certain stages in her journey.

How to Find a Great Job
https://medium.com/@gibsonbiddle/how-to-find-a-great-job-944caa29c980
This is the story of how a guy named Gibson Biddle landed the role of VP of Product at Netflix after being out of work for two years. A great read that's worth your time.

Also Recommended: Stay up to date about an ATS like iCIMS at the following blog:
https://www.icims.com/hiring-insights/blog/all/

Hire Expectations Institute Blog is published by iCIMS, which is one of the largest Applicant Tracking Systems out there and is used by brand-name companies like Amazon, FedEx, and H&R Block. iCIMS stands for Internet Collaborative Information Management System.

Conclusion: A Cup of Tea with Bruce Lee

Now that you've studied these resume strategies, you're all set, right? Ready to skydive into the job hunt? I'm glad you're pumped, but don't get too comfortable and assume that your work is over.

Depending on where you are in your search, it may take time to land the interview that you want. You'll need to do a bit of networking and outreach within the industry and with the companies that interest you. Remember that your resume is just one component of your search. Your chances dramatically improve when you have an inside advocate. Keep a positive attitude, don't let rejection letters, ignored applications/emails or other people's perceptions of your value get in the way of your goal.

There is a concept in Zen Buddhism called Shoshin (初心) which means "beginner's mind." It requires you to leave behind any preconceived notions of the subject and approach it with curiosity, openness, and a bit of excitement, just as a beginner would. Viewing your job search process with fresh eyes will cultivate new thoughts and approaches for you that an expert wouldn't consider.

With that in mind, consider this story by famed martial artist Bruce Lee:

> *A university professor was searching for a master of Zen Buddhism to help him study. When the professor arrived, the Zen master offered him a cup of tea, which the professor graciously accepted. As they spoke, the Zen master continued to pour tea into the professor's cup until*

it overflowed. The professor said, 'Sorry, but the cup is overflowing.' The Zen master replied, 'Oh, you noticed. To fit in any more you must first empty your cup.'[69]

So let's empty our minds of any limiting beliefs and approach your resume with a beginner's mind. I'm giving you a bit of leverage. Take what you will and make it your own.

"Most of us believe our work should speak for itself — it doesn't. How we market and sell ourselves comes into play long before we get the opportunity to prove ourselves through our work."
— Jay Samit, Disrupt You!

Keep Your Focus

Remember, this is a marketing campaign, which means that it's going to take effort and focus on your part. I don't want you to just skim the words. No, I need you to stay positive, remove distractions, and keep your focus. J.K. Rowling didn't passively write her bestselling Harry Potter series between checking her Facebook and responding to notifications on her phone. She locked herself in a hotel room and stayed away from distractions until she finished writing. Distractions are everywhere. Multitasking, which is our default state, kills productivity. It's vital that you provide your mind with the mental bandwidth to be able to focus on your resume and your goals.

---

[69] The Only Sales Guide You'll Ever Need by Anthony Iannarino

Even then, after you have carved out time to concentrate your energy, your work won't be complete. As I've mentioned before, the blueprint for landing a job in today's market has changed. You will realize big wins through a series of small wins: this book, your resume, your attitude, and outlook are all small wins as you get ready to land your job.

In the future, the traditional resume will be replaced by your portfolio, branding, and performance reputation. Futurists from the Institute for the Future tell us that the job hunt will be about curating your online reputation.

Consider these powerful points about the future in a recent report on the changing nature of work:

> *Managing reputation will be knowing how to protect, trade, donate, and reap your own value from data about you is how you'll manage your reputation and build your personal brand—and learning how to curate your brand in multiple media and many cultures will be the key to success.*

> *[W]ork will evolve from individual hiring and roles to hiring of teams and team production... work will focus more on work roles than jobs, because the tasks that need to be performed will change on a regular basis.*

> *[I]n the future we will be moving from resumes to reputations for talent recruitment.*[70]

[70] 'AI Forces Shaping Work & Learning in 2030: Report on Expert Convenings for a New Work+ Learn Future.' Institute for the Future, October 2018.
http://www.iftf.org/fileadmin/user_upload/images/ourwork/Work___Learn/IFTF_Lumina_AI_Forces_Work_Learn_101218.pdf

Where you place your bets (spend your time) matters

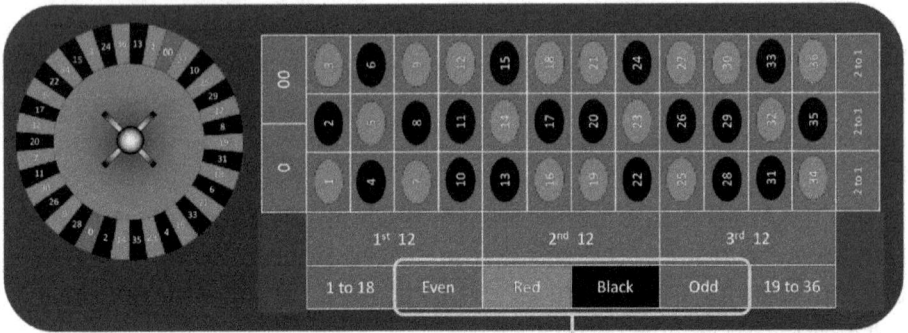

Some recent grads can be passive when first starting out by submitting dozens of their copy-and-pasted resumes thinking they've been productive. So they take a break and wait to hear back. This strategy does not lend itself to success. This is similar to making passive bets in the game of roulette.

Rather you should spend your time accordingly to make strategic bets

30% of Your Time	70% of Your Time
1) Reach out to your 1st level connections on LinkedIn 2) Write blog posts to boost your SEO (Search Engine Optimization) of your LinkedIn profile	1) Network at industry events 2) Do your homework on a handful of companies that you want to work for and creating a competitive analysis or brief / case study of your past performance 3) Study the careers, backgrounds, and interests of the hiring managers you aim to work for 4) Before you even apply invite the hiring manager to a brief cup of coffee

Beyond the Secrets: Bonus Strategies

Check Your Social Media & Dating Apps

Before diving into dating apps and social media, do yourself a favor and Google your name to see what's currently showing up. And, if you haven't done so already, go to Google alerts and put in an alert for your name so that you're alerted by email anytime your name comes up.

If you use any social media like Facebook, Twitter, or Instagram and you have any posts or items that aren't pristine or professional, go ahead and do yourself a favor by either cleaning up your post or locking your profile privacy down. Use free social media monitoring tools like SumAll.com to capture mentions that Google Alerts fails to grab.

If you use any dating apps that are linked to your Facebook account and you have anything on them that might be remotely questionable, lock it down. A good idea is to unlink these apps from your Facebook and sign up separately with a different email account. It is worth knowing that larger companies do not have a problem with entering your name into one of their social platforms to scrap any data about you (FullContact, ContentBomb, Connect6, Discoveryly, Rapporto, 360 Social, and UVA).

"Unlike traditional hiring tools such as interviews and contacting past employers, social media sites hold out the promise of revealing the 'real' job applicant," said Les Rosen, an attorney and the CEO of Employment Screening Resources, a background screening firm based in the San Francisco area."[71]

---

[71] Maurer, Roy. "HR Weeds Out Applicants" on SHRM.org

Additionally, companies are also using tools like Fama.io to apply machine learning to scan public content online while layering that with internal HR policies and heuristics to see which candidates and current employees might be a risk to their brand, culture, and overall productivity.

70% of employers are snooping candidates' social media profiles

By Lauren Salm | June 15, 2017   Share: 🅕 🅘🅝 🅣

You're being watched: Don't forget that your social media accounts are accessible to potential employers.
(Image source: https://www.careerbuilder.com/advice/social-media-survey-2017)

The following states in the table below have social media privacy laws which prevent employers from asking for your social media credentials in considering employment: [72]

---

[72] http://www.ncsl.org/research/telecommunications-and-information-technology/state-laws-prohibiting-access-to-social-media-usernames-and-passwords.aspx

Arkansas	California	Colorado	Connecticut	Delaware
Illinois	Louisiana	Maine	Maryland	Michigan
Montana	Nebraska	Nevada	New Hampshire	New Jersey
New Mexico	Oklahoma	Oregon	Rhode Island	Tennessee
Utah	Vermont	Virginia	Washington	West Virginia
Wisconsin	District of Columbia	Guam		

Despite laws existing in many states, this doesn't stop employers from searching for your posts that are public: This is treated as public information to further evaluate a candidate. If your future employer asks you for your username and password, thank them for the opportunity and then move on. That's none of their business, and there needs to be boundaries.

No call back? Or the email saying, "Thank you for your interest"?

During my own job hunts, there were plenty of times when—even though I knew in my soul that I was the best candidate—I received an email response like this one:

Hi [name],

Thanks for the time and effort to apply to ACME! While we regret that we won't be moving forward with you in this role, we want you to continue exploring a career path at ACME. New positions are always opening up, and we encourage you to find other roles that match your skills and experience. Please visit ACME Careers to view current opportunities.

You can follow us on LinkedIn, Facebook, Instagram, or Twitter to be alerted of the latest company news.

Thank you for being a part of the ACME community, and for your interest in the role.

Sincerely,

The ACME People Operations Team

Even after reading this book, following the rules, making adjustments, and doing everything right … the painful reality is that you may receive emails similar to this one and not get a call back. This is not your fault. Here's why:

1) Depending on the industry and job, the posting you applied for was already filled internally by someone else, and that means you never had a chance. But sometimes because of policies and union contracts, the company is required to publicly post the role without regard for candidates.

2) Sudden budget cuts, hiring freezes, or departmental layoffs have put the posted position into jeopardy.

3) Some companies simply drag their feet because that's how they operate.

4) The role was filled months ago, yet someone within the organization forgot to pull the posting down.

Despite all of these possible explanations, it is still worth getting someone on the phone who is familiar with your candidacy to ask if you should apply again in the future (you're not calling to dispute the decision) and how you can improve your candidacy. State that you'd be grateful to receive any feedback along those lines. It is rare that anyone will be dismissive in the face of a plea for helpful feedback.

Shortening Your Links

If you're unable to get a customized domain name for your website or your LinkedIn profile, use a URL shortened with ow.ly, Google's shortener https://goo.gl, or Bitly's, which can be a bit more customized at https://bitly.com.

Analyze Personalities

Use the Chrome browser plugin Crystal Knows to analyze the personalities of the people you're trying to contact. Crystal Knows can check any LinkedIn profile based on the DISC (Dominance-Influence-Conscientiousness-Steadiness) personality classifier. The plugin will provide tips on how you can work with potential contacts. Upgraded plans provide guidance on the best way to reach out when connecting with a new contact.

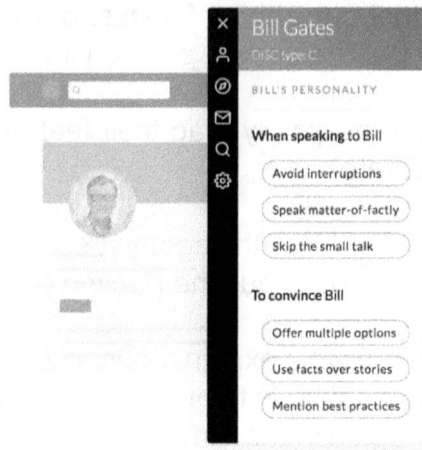

See how your social personality stacks up

To do this, check out the following: https://frrole.ai/deepsense-app/

The AI from DeepSense goes a bit further beyond Crystal Knows and scrapes your social media to analyze your behavioral strengths and weaknesses based upon the DISC personality methodology.

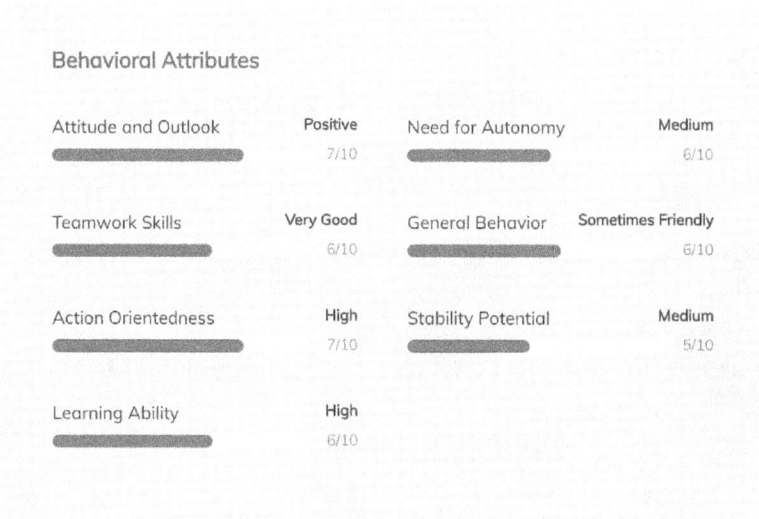

Behavioral Attributes

Attitude and Outlook	Positive 7/10	Need for Autonomy	Medium 6/10
Teamwork Skills	Very Good 6/10	General Behavior	Sometimes Friendly 6/10
Action Orientedness	High 7/10	Stability Potential	Medium 5/10
Learning Ability	High 6/10		

(Image source: https://frrole.ai/deepsense-app)

Although AI is in its infancy, it's only a matter of time before it analyzes enough profiles to start self-correcting and spit out a well-calibrated analysis.

Email Investigation

You've submitted your resume into the black hole of a database. Great. Rather than let your resume remain dormant, you need to reach out to the hiring manager, or, better yet, an employee at the company. How do you do that? Often the job description will say whom the role reports to or the department the role falls under. If it doesn't, then you'll need to do a little research by either calling HR or using LinkedIn to see who would likely be the hiring manager based on their title. Hiring managers want to see grit in their candidates. Once you've identified who that might be, these three browser plug-ins can help you track down their email addresses and, in many cases, their phone numbers. As of the writing of this book, all three have basic fee plans available:

https://discover.ly/

https://contactout.com/

https://hunter.io/

All plug-ins work best with Chrome browsers and integrate with LinkedIn.

When those run out then will you want to check out these two:

https://Anymailfinder.com

www.Verifyemailaddress.org

Once you're able to reach a hiring manager and they've agreed to schedule a phone call, it's a lot easier to use a platform like Calendly that integrates with multiple systems rather than email back-and-forth to determine availability.

https://calendly.com/

Jobs For Veterans

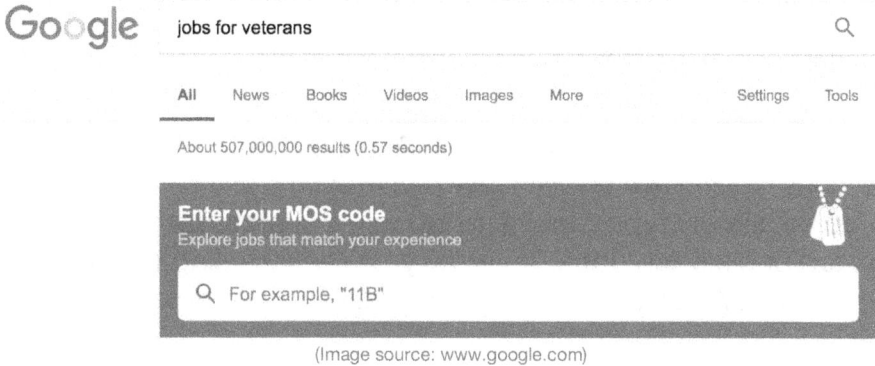

(Image source: www.google.com)

Now members of the military and veterans can type *"jobs for veterans"* in Google and enter in their occupational specialty code or MOS code to see job postings which correlate similar skills from the job posting to their jobs and experience in the military.

Job Search Sites

Although there are plenty of sites out there to choose from, I'd suggest sticking to the following three: LinkedIn, Angellist, ZipRecruiter, and Indeed. Stay away from job postings that are more than 12 weeks old. Also, Google now offers a way to aggregate your search by setting alerts and pulling job descriptions from employers and career sites across the web. As soon as the job descriptions (JDs) are published, they're added to the listing.

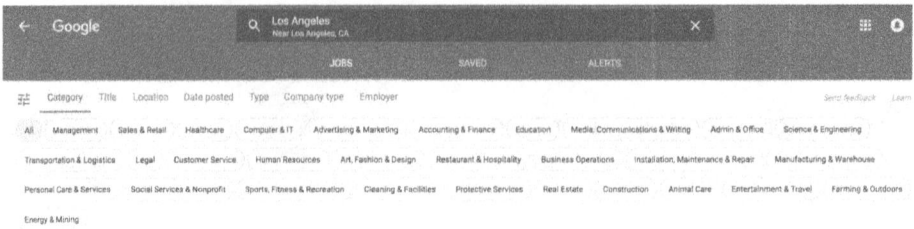

(Image source: www.google.com)

To do so, simply type "Job" into Google's search bar. In the blue box tap or click on "Jobs." Narrow your results using the filter as seen above. A key benefit is seeing possible commute times as well.

If you're looking to apply to startups, then I'd suggest AngelList: https://Angel.co/jobs

In addition, if you're looking outside of the United States, https://whoishiring.io/ aggregates startup jobs around the world.

After you've reviewed the startup landscape, you might read the following by Harj Taggar:

How to Choose a Startup to Work For by Thinking Like An Investor
https://triplebyte.com/blog/how-to-choose-a-startup-to-work-for

Identity Theft

Consider a few thoughts about identity theft related to your resume: For starters, be selective of who gets to see your resume. As previously mentioned, do not list your mailing address on your resume. It's perfectly okay to get around geographical prejudice by listing the metropolitan city you're currently in or where you will be relocating. Identity theft can happen fairly easily if someone is so inclined with your address, name, and date of birth. Your information can be matched to any of the number of data breaches that have taken place.

World's Biggest Data Breaches & Hacks

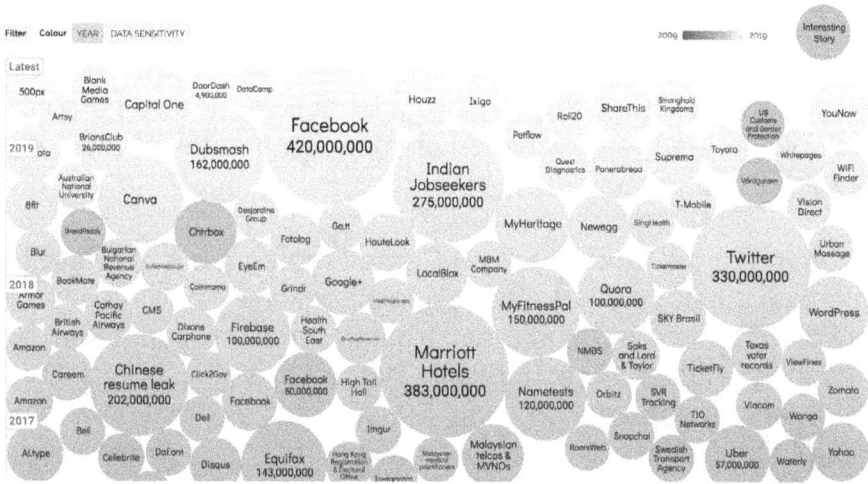

(Image source: https://www.informationisbeautiful.net/visualizations/worlds-biggest-data-breaches-hacks)

An additional piece of content to guard are the years of your education to prevent a thief from guessing your age. One may think that removing the dates of your education from your resume implies that a candidate is hiding something. When you graduated isn't highly relevant: your education is. So if a recruiter or hiring manager really wants to know when you obtained your degree, he or she can ask you in your interview.

Final Thoughts

Well, we're near the end of the book, congratulations are in order. I hope I was able to provide you with fresh tools, secrets, and strategies to get you to the next stage and fulfill my earlier prediction that I'd change the way you look at resumes. I'm confident that I did even though I won't bother asking. Cocky? No. Confident? Yes. 😎 But it's all about mindset, right? The fact that you even made it this far says a lot about you as a person. You now have a greater chance of implementing the strategies contained in this book.

According to the Pew Research Center, more than a quarter of American adults had not read a single book in 2019.[73] Meaning they didn't thumb through a paperback, scroll through a Kindle, or even listen to an audiobook. It's not just practical books like this. Even the popular book *Fifty Shades of Grey* went unread by 75% of those who bought it.[74] Imagine that.

So, here is the thing, now that you have a solid resume or at least know how to create one, you still need to land an offer. That's the place where this book stops. Despite your timeline and the industry that you're targeting, the resume is one step in the process. Your brand and how well you interview will determine the decision to hire you. The great thing about creating your resume, though, is that it forces you to think very specifically about your professional qualities, and that will help you prepare for your interview. If you still find that you're stuck after using all the tools in this book, you're welcome to get more in depth with the resources at my site www.ResumeSecretsBook.com. And should you want to work with me on your strategy, just know that

---

[73] https://www.pewresearch.org/fact-tank/2019/09/26/who-doesnt-read-books-in-america/

[74] https://www.wsj.com/articles/the-summers-most-unread-book-is-1404417569

I'm interested in clients who are highly motivated and qualified, which produces results.

My hope is that you will move outside of any safety bubble you're currently in and change your mindset. Your results are directly predicated upon your mindset and taking action. I've been through it, and the students I work with have been through it, too; my goal is to pull them out of it.

There are thousands of companies out there that have no idea who you are or that they need your skills and invaluable help to reach *their* goals. When businesses fail it is more often than not a problem stemming from sales and marketing... the same is true for you as a brand. You have to put yourself out there. Then, when you do, make sure to follow up. Be diligent about your follow-up. I rarely see that happen. The longer you sit and stare at your email, hoping for a response, the more out of touch and frustrated you'll become.

If you produced an amazing project or result and you believe in what you did and are damn proud of it, you had better tell people that you think so. That means emailing them, connecting on LinkedIn, and getting them on the phone to sell yourself. At worst you'll gain a no, and at best you may get an interview, a piece of feedback, a new contact, or a suggestion of who to speak with next.

A roadblock simply means that there is more growth ahead and more to learn. Resist the email rejections and resist the complacency to let up. I want you to succeed, and I believe in you!

What is even more important than my belief in you is *your* belief in yourself. Others see in us what we see in ourselves, and you will discover that this is true during your interview. Your confidence and powerful belief in your own value will be felt by the hiring committee, the hiring manager, and others around you. Look at all of the wonderful things you say about yourself on your resume and follow this simple two-word rule: *Believe them.*

If you commit to the secrets I've laid out for you in this book, I know you will soon be sending me a success story. Your passion and commitment to improve yourself not only will open up new opportunities, it will change you. Good luck on your journey. I'll leave you with the following quote:

> *The more aligned you are with the things you want the more powerfully you attract them. The things you congruently want have no choice but to be attracted to you. People who are congruent are attractive, magnetic—even charismatic. When you are fully congruent, you are irresistible.* [75]

I wish you congruency to your goals, interviews, and job offers and that you have tremendous success throughout your career.

Sincerely,

Chris
ResumeSecretsBook@gmail.com

P.s.
If you found this book to be helpful in any way I would be grateful for your review on Amazon. Thank you in advance!

---

[75] The One Minute Millionaire by Mark Victor Hansen and Robert G. Allen

Access additional content at:
www.ResumeSecretsBook.com

Acknowledgements

Front cover photo used under license from Shutterstock.com
Front and back cover design by: TopHills of 99Designs
Photo credit: Syda Productions
https://www.shutterstock.com/g/dolgachov
Photo ID: 364671062

Headshot photo: Mark Dust Photography www.markdust.com

This book was a true team effort, not just polishing the rough edges, but also in editing, organizing content, and reworking examples to make a point stick. If this book helps one recent graduate then we did our jobs. I must express my gratitude to everyone who helped make this book come to reality... directly or indirectly.

Jay Samit – As someone who is inspired by your work I'm still in awe of your foreword. I couldn't have asked for such a thought provoking piece let alone the credibility. Your book *Disrupt You!* is one I constantly cite and review, so it's truly an honor to have you grace the first pages of this book. You're both a visionary and a thought leader, and I eagerly look forward to seeing what you put out next. I sincerely can't thank you enough for your support. A heartfelt thank you - and yes I will be paying it forward.

Ross McPherson, you've been a guiding light and I've learned a ton from you. You taught me about what not to do and what worked to get me interviews and, eventually, the jobs I wanted.

John Suarez, the trainer of trainers. Thank you for your help and for sharing your wisdom.

Jason Barquero - thank you for always being supportive, sharing resources, and bringing in the best and brightest. John Baker your CVS receipt costume is priceless. I hope you extend the trend in other creative ways. Thank you Mark F. Schaefer for allowing me to share an excerpt of your book, KNOWN. You're a marketing wizard that I continue to learn from.

Bernie Jaworski, your mentorship has been invaluable. You're the grand master of business chess. Your advice is always timeless and spot on. Thank you for always being there.

Nick Owchar, the many revisions - I can't thank you enough for helping take a boring topic and make it fun and practical. Also, Brianna Soloski, Dr. Jorge Barraza, Joseph Sahili, Julia Baumgaertner, Steven Dunbar, Jonathan Shearer, Kimberley Diaz, Thanh Lu, Mark Sudell, and Dr. Melinda Harriman - thank you for editing, proofreading, and your overall feedback.

Nancy Soni, Tony Hammon, Destini Lone Elk, and Martha Curioni - thank you for chatting with me and helping me refine my thinking.

Thank you to Mark Anderson of Andertoons.com. Your sketches liven up an otherwise dull topic.